HOW TO STUDY LITERATURE
General Editors: John Peck and Mar

HOW TO STUDY MILTON

IN THE SAME SERIES

HOW TO STUDY MILTON

David Kearns

MACMILLAN

First published 1993 by
THE MACMILLAN PRESS LTD
Houndmills, Basingstoke, Hampshire RG21 2XS
and London
Companies and representatives
throughout the world

ISBN 0–333–54911–2

A catalogue record for this book is available
from the British Library

Copy-edited and typeset by Cairns Craig Editorial, Edinburgh

Printed in China

To
Janice and Alexandra
and
Shantung, Chiang Mai and Grimalkin

Contents

General Editor's preface

Everybody who studies literature, either for an examination or simply for pleasure, experiences the same problem: how to understand and respond to the text. As every student of literature knows, it is perfectly possible to read a book over and over again and yet still feel baffled and at a loss as to what to say about it. One answer to this problem, of course, is to accept someone else's view of the text, but how much more rewarding it would be if you could work out your own critical response to any book you choose or are required to study.

The aim of this series is to help you develop your critical skills by offering practical advice about how to read, understand and analyse literature. Each volume provides you with a clear method of study so that you can see how to set about tackling texts on your own. While the authors of each volume approach the problem in a different way, every book in the series attempts to provide you with some broad ideas about the kind of texts you are likely to be studying and some broad ideas about how to think about literature; each volume then shows you how to apply these ideas in a way which should help you construct your own analysis and interpretation. Unlike most critical books, therefore, the books in this series do not simply convey someone else's thinking about a text, but encourage you and show you how to think about a text for yourself.

Each book is written with an awareness that you are likely to be preparing for an examination, and therefore practical advice is given not only on how to understand and analyse literature, but also on how to organise a written response. Our hope is that, although these books are intended to serve a practical purpose, they may also enrich your enjoyment of literature by making you a more confident reader, alert to the interest and pleasure to be derived from literary texts.

John Peck
Martin Coyle

Acknowledgements

I would like to thank the general editors of this series who have been immensely patient as this book has slowly come into being. Martin Coyle's encouragement and cajoling have kept me going on many occasions, and John Peck's surgical eye with matters of style and syntax have cleared out many potential errors.

I must thank the many students who have suffered this text in various forms and gone away claiming to have had insight into Milton's writing. Perhaps, most of all, I owe a debt to Catherine Belsey, whose book about Milton opened up new channels of exploration in the work of one of my favourite authors.

Introduction

Milton lived from 1608 to 1674. During that time England experienced a Civil War between 1642 and 1646, the execution of its monarch, Charles I, in 1649, a short period of republican government, under Oliver Cromwell, from 1649 to 1660, and the restoration of the monarchy with the return of Charles II in 1660. In Chapter 3 of this book I will fill out the historical details of these events so that you can set Milton's writing in context and see how it is caught up in the debates and issues of its time. My first aim in these pages, however, is to show you how, by using a few simple ideas, you can build your own analysis of a Milton poem. In particular, although I shall look at other poems later on, I am going to concentrate on *Paradise Lost*, an epic poem in twelve books. This is Milton's major work and is very often set for examinations, although students usually find themselves studying just one or two books from it. This raises an obvious question. How do you deal with only a part of a long work? Two points will help answer this straight away. First, you do have to have an idea of the poem as a whole so that you can see how it all fits together, and I will be offering you that below. Second, you may find it helpful to think of each book as a 'chapter'. That immediately makes *Paradise Lost* seem more manageable, but it will also remind you that the events in the 'chapter' you are studying lead on to other events and so are part of a larger pattern. Let me start, though, with a summary of the whole poem.

Paradise Lost tells the story of the fall of man. According to Biblical accounts of creation, God first made man and woman as perfect creatures. God had forbidden the man and woman, called Adam and Eve, to eat the fruit of the tree of the knowledge of good and evil, but Eve was persuaded to eat this fruit by a serpent and she then persuaded Adam to do likewise. As a result, they were expelled from the garden in Eden which God had created as a paradise for them, and became mortal creatures, subject to death. Traditionally, the serpent in the garden is identified with the figure of Satan, who led a force of angels in a failed rebellion against God in Heaven. Satan and his allies were punished by being sent to Hell, created for them as a place of endless torture and misery. From Hell, Satan plotted his revenge against God, which he achieved by bringing about the downfall of Adam and Eve.

Milton's poem begins immediately after the defeat of the rebel angels, describing their situation and their plotting of revenge in the first three Books. In the fourth Book, Satan arrives in Eden and we are introduced to Adam and Eve. The next four Books are concerned with an account by the archangel Raphael of the war in Heaven and God's subsequent creation of the world, stressing the danger Adam may have to face from Satan. Adam also describes his first meeting with Eve. In Books IX and X Milton recounts the central story of the fall of Adam and Eve as well as telling of their subsequent repentance. The final two Books are a prophetic account, given by the archangel Michael, of the effects that the Fall will have on the history of the human race, and in particular the way in which they will be redeemed by God's son, Jesus.

In order to understand what is happening in Milton's poem, we need to detect some sort of pattern or basic idea. It is in fact fairly easy to see that the story tells of the conflict between the forces of good (God, the archangels) and the forces of evil (Satan, the fallen angels). This fundamental conflict, or *tension*, underpins the whole of *Paradise Lost*, and will provide us with a simple way of coming to terms with its details. Another way of putting this basic conflict is to talk about a tension between order on the one hand, with God's positive creative actions, and chaos on the other, with Satan's negative, destructive actions. God creates, Satan destroys. God or good is a positive force, Satan or evil is a negative force and the two are constantly opposed. Indeed, this tension between negative and positive exists even in the title of the poem with the good, *Paradise*, subjected to the evil of being *Lost*.

These ideas, good and evil, order and chaos, positive and negative, are our key to the reading of the poem, they are its large themes. The first – good and evil – is perhaps the central one. By keeping this tension constantly in mind, we can approach the poem knowing that we are looking for the ways in which ideas about good and evil are set against each other. The other tensions I have mentioned arise from or are the result of this central conflict, and as your reading becomes more confident you will see that there are further tensions, perhaps more complex, which appear in the text. All the time, however, you should be thinking of good versus evil as the point from which to begin.

Keeping this broad idea in mind will give you a hold on the text. What you will also need, however, is a method of analysis for working on the text, and this I will be demonstrating in the following chapters. Basically this involves looking at a number of passages and seeing how they reflect the broad issues of the poem. The method I will be using involves six steps. First, I will summarise the events in each Book, trying to find a broad pattern so that I get an overall idea of it. Next I take a sequence of four passages where I look closely at the text, and then, finally, in step six, I try to see what I have achieved. This is the key to the method – each step takes you on a stage further as you build up your ideas. As you will see later, I also offer you a way of analyzing the passages you choose which involves a further series of smaller stages. The method, then, is to see how the broad theme of a poem is always present in its details, and how those details in turn give us a more concrete and complex sense of the theme.

I shall use this method in the next two chapters for Books I and II of *Paradise Lost* as a way in, because even if you are not studying these books, this is the sensible place to start with Milton. Then comes a chapter sketching in the historical background. After this I shall be dealing with (in examination terms) the most 'popular' books of the poem, Books IV, IX and X. Once you have grasped the method you should be able to apply it to any book. Later, I shall be adapting the method slightly in order to give you an approach to Milton's 'minor' poems, and to *Samson Agonistes*. Again, let me repeat that whether you are interested in one or two books of *Paradise Lost*, or in all of it or none of it, you should read through the next couple of chapters so that you can see how this method of reading Milton works.

1

Paradise Lost, Book I

Constructing an overall analysis

In this chapter I am going to analyse Book I of *Paradise Lost* using the method I have just outlined. As I said in the Introduction, we can best approach *Paradise Lost* to start with by looking at the ways in which ideas about good and evil are set against each other. Central to the Book is Satan, a powerful figure of evil who repels and attracts in almost equal measure, inspiring fear and disgust in the reader because of his foolhardy and unnecessary arrogance in refusing to accept defeat, yet gaining our sympathy for his apparent desire to pursue what he believes to be a just cause in the face of overwhelming odds. We need to try to understand the character of Satan and how his role operates in the context of the conflict between good and evil.

Book I of *Paradise Lost* contains 798 lines of verse. That may well be more lines of poetry than you have ever previously read, and may seem rather daunting. In the opening stages of your reading of the poem, however, it is best simply to set aside the fear of reading such a bulk of poetry. Take the text and read it through as quickly as you can. Do not worry about things that may appear incomprehensible, and certainly do not get bogged down in reading notes and glosses. 'What is happening now?' is a good question constantly to ask yourself; but do not be concerned if that does not become immediately obvious. You will need several further readings to ensure a fuller understanding that will set you up ready for the first step in your analysis.

1 *After reading the text, think about the story and what kind of pattern you can see in it*

The first step in our analysis is to try and see the text as a whole.

This will obviously be easier if we have a clear sense of what happens in Book I. What we need is a good summary of the text to work from. To a limited extent, we already have that in the poem itself. Look in your text. At some point, usually immediately before the poem begins, you will find a longish paragraph headed 'The Argument'. In seventeenth-century terms, that means the 'plot', the sequence of events, which is what we are after. Let us look at the *Argument* for Book I (the text I will be working from is the Oxford Standard Authors *Milton Poetical Works*, edited by Douglas Bush):

> This first Book initially proposes, in brief, the whole subject, Man's disobedience, and the loss thereupon of Paradise, wherein he was placed: then touches the prime cause of his fall, the Serpent, or rather Satan in the Serpent; who revolting from God, and drawing to his side many legions of angels, was by the command of God driven out of Heaven with all his crew into the great deep. Which action passed over, the poem hastes into the midst of things, presenting Satan with his angels now fallen into Hell – described here, not in the centre (for heaven and earth may be supposed as yet not made, certainly not yet accursed) but in a place of utter darkness, fitliest called Chaos. Here Satan with his angels lying on the burning lake, thunderstruck and aston-ished, after a certain space recovers, as from confusion; calls up him who, next in order and dignity, lay by him; they confer of their miserable fall. Satan awakens all his legions, who lay till then in the same manner confounded. They rise: their numbers, array of battle, their chief leaders named, according to the idols known afterwards in Canaan and the countries adjoining. To these Satan directs his speech, comforts them with hope yet of regaining heaven, but tells them lastly of a new world and new kind of creature to be created, according to an ancient prophecy or report in heaven, for that angels were long before this visible creation was the opinion of many ancient fathers. To find out the truth of this prophecy, and what to determine thereon, he refers to a full council. What his associates thence attempt. Pandemonium, the palace of Satan, rises, suddenly built out of the deep; the infernal peers there sit in council.   (pp. 211–12)

Some of that may be a little hazy, but it is worth reading over several times because it is so helpful – it gives us all sorts of details. But that is also its problem. As I have already told you, the dominant factor in this Book is Satan, the principal situation is Hell. If you find the Argument too difficult to follow at this stage, I suggest you try out the following.

In your reading of Book I you may have noticed that the verse is split into paragraphs. A very simple summary of the content of each of these verse paragraphs will give you a fairly accurate summary of the whole of the Book. Apart from very minor linking phrases, there are twenty-one paragraph divisions in this Book, which may be summarised as follows:

1. Invocation to the Heavenly Muses.
2. Cause of Adam and Eve's fall, attributed to the Serpent; his sin and punishment.
3. Satan in Hell; description of Hell – light/dark stressed; his companions, particularly Beelzebub; Satan first named at line 82.
4. Satan's first speech.
5. Beelzebub's response to Satan.
6. Satan's second speech.
7. Description of Satan's 'physicality' – good and evil contrasted.
8. Satan stands up, travels to 'dry land', followed by Beelzebub.
9. Satan's third speech.
10. Beelzebub's second response.
11. Satan described as he moves 'toward the shore'; he approaches his legions on the burning lake.
12. Satan's fourth speech.
13. The fallen angels rise up – their numbers are stressed; they send out their 'heads and leaders'; their lack of a name – erased from Heaven's records, not yet given names by humans.
14. Invocation to the Muse to name them.
15. The list of the main fallen angels with their pagan names.
16. The lesser figures are grouped together.
17. The troops are rallied, they form up in military manner; Satan inspects their ranks; comparison of these with human – i.e. lesser – armies; return to Satan and his place at the head of these figures.

18.   Satan's fifth speech.
19.   The angels respond by clashing swords on shields.
20.   The building of Pandemonium.
21.   The angels are called to a council at Pandemonium which is about to begin as the Book closes.

I am more confident of this summary because it is something that has arisen from my own reading. Satan and Hell predominate. Does the summary show us an 'opening chapter'? The answer would appear to be yes. The principal characters are announced, namely God and Satan, together with their respective current situations, Heaven and Hell. The summary also introduces Man and the Serpent, as well as the Earth. You should, though, be able to see that the summary in itself is not particularly helpful until we have gained control of it by finding that central tension we are looking for. In this case, the task is relatively simple as Satan represents evil and God represents good. The summary presents the fundamental conflict of the text – a fallen Satan, a victorious God. You will also see that there is evidence of other, perhaps more complex, tensions. For example, the summary also broaches the idea of 'Man's disobedience' against God, a further source of tension in the poem, and one which makes the poem far more interesting to its readers, who are, of course, human! Now, let us try to see how this central tension, the conflict between good and evil, provides a pattern with which we can examine individual passages in Book I.

2   *Select a short passage for discussion and try to build on the ideas you have established so far*

If you look closely at the verse paragraph summary, you will see that certain of the paragraphs more obviously than others deal with the central tension between good and evil. The first one that does so is Paragraph 3 in which we find Hell described by means of a stress upon light and dark. Light and dark, it is worth remembering, are often used in literature to present an image of good and evil. Since this paragraph also concerns Satan it will be a useful point at which to begin an examination of the text:

Nine times the space that measures day and night
To mortal men, he with his horrid crew
Lay vanquished, rolling in the fiery gulf
Confounded though immortal. But his doom
Reserved him to more wrath; for now the thought
Both of lost happiness and lasting pain
Torments him; round he throws his baleful eyes,
That witnessed huge affliction and dismay
Mixed with obdurate pride and steadfast hate.
At once as far as Angels ken he views
The dismal situation waste and wild:
A dungeon horrible, on all sides round
As one great furnace flamed, yet from those flames
No light, but rather darkness visible
Served only to discover sights of woe,
Regions of sorrow, doleful shades, where peace
And rest can never dwell, hope never comes
That comes to all; but torture without end
Still urges, and a fiery deluge, fed
With ever-burning sulphur unconsumed:
Such place Eternal Justice had prepared
For those rebellious, here their prison ordained
In utter darkness, and their portion set
As far removed from God and light of heav'n
As from the centre thrice to th' utmost pole.
O how unlike the place from whence they fell!
                              (Book I, ll. 50–75)

A passage like this may seem to present many problems: the sentences are long, the order of the words is sometimes unexpected, and some of the vocabulary is complex. The general drift, however, is reasonably clear: we are presented with a picture of Satan and his fallen angels in Hell. But what do we say about this? The idea we have to work with is that we should be able to find the large themes of the poem in every passage we consider. Here, for example, it is clear that Satan and his fellow angels are rebels. They have been condemned as criminals as the result of some crime committed against their previous society. What we see, therefore, is a conflict between an idea of the well-balanced society and those who oppose it, who are evil.

Deservedly, they are in Hell. And what characterises Hell is that, as this passage shows, it lacks things: it lacks light, there is only the appalling 'darkness visible'. It is 'far removed from God and light of Heaven'.

In responding to the passage, then, we can work on the order versus chaos opposition, and see how the passage reinforces this idea with its light versus dark opposition. But there are more details to be considered. Satan is a figure in torment because of the 'happiness' he has lost and the 'pain' he now suffers, but although he sees 'huge affliction and dismay', he still displays 'obdurate pride and steadfast hate'. His evil nature is heavily stressed; he shows no remorse for his actions. What we might also notice is that Milton uses some curiously paradoxical phrases to describe Satan, such as 'confounded though immortal' and that he puts words like 'happiness' and 'pain' close together. It is a way of writing that repeatedly brings to the fore the whole idea of the large conflicts, especially that between good and evil, that motivates the entire poem.

3 Select a second passage for discussion

I will select my second passage by returning to my verse paragraph summary. Shortly after the passage we have just explored, you will see that paragraph 7 again mentions Satan, but that it also mentions that good and evil are contrasted. This is a sensible place to go for further examination of the central conflict we are concerned with.

> Thus Satan talking to his nearest mate
> With head uplift above the wave, and eyes
> That sparkling blazed; his other parts besides
> Prone on the flood, extended long and large
> Lay floating many a rood, in bulk as huge
> As whom the fables name of monstrous size,
> Titanian or Earth-born, that warred on Jove,
> Briareos or Typhon, whom the den
> By ancient Tarsus held, or that sea-beast
> Leviathan, which God of all his works

Created hugest that swim th' ocean stream:
Him haply slumb'ring on the Norway foam,
The pilot of some small night-foundered skiff,
Deeming some island, oft, as seamen tell,
With fixed anchor in his scaly rind
Moors by his side under the lee, while night
Invests the sea, and wished morn delays:
So stretched out huge in length the Arch-Fiend lay
Chained on the burning lake; nor ever thence
Had ris'n or heaved his head, but that the will
And high permission of all-ruling Heaven
Left him at large to his own dark designs,
That with reiterated crimes he might
Heap on himself damnation, while he sought
Evil to others, and enraged might see
How all his malice served but to bring forth
Infinite goodness, grace and mercy shown
On man by him seduced, but on himself
Treble confusion, wrath and vengeance poured.
(Book I, ll. 192–220)

When I examined the first passage, you may have been wondering how I actually ordered my approach. This time I will break down my material into a number of individual stages so that the method becomes clearer to you. The stages will separate out each of my points of enquiry so that you can see how to do it yourself and how to push your analysis forward gradually. Notice that the point of these stages is to relate the detail of the text to your grasp of its larger meaning, but also to use the detail to refine your grasp of that meaning. It is a two-way process – detail and larger ideas all the time interacting. Here are the stages:

a)   Make a short statement of what the passage is about.
b)   Search for an opposition or tension within the passage.
c)   Analyse the details of the passage, relating them to the opposition already noted.
d)   Try to say how the passage relates to the Book as a whole.
e)   Search for anything distinctive about the passage, particularly in the area of style, which you have not already noted.

a)   *Make a short statement of what the passage is about*
This passage has two aims. First, it attempts to give the reader some idea of Satan's physical size; second, it reinforces the picture of him as the personification of evil.

b)   *Search for an opposition or tension within the passage*
The second half of this passage returns to the conflict we saw in the first passage. Here the tension between Satan and God is proposed as a conflict between 'wills' – Satan is apparently left 'at large to his own dark designs': can you see how, as in the first passage we looked at, the idea of dark is by far the most frequently employed method of describing Satan's behaviour? But there is a complication: Satan might appear to be challenging God, but God is very much in control, for Satan is only allowed to get away with what he does through the 'high permission of all-ruling Heaven'. It is as if God, as the source of good, has a larger plan for the world, that Satan's evil will ultimately contribute to the sum total of good in the world by allowing God to show His 'grace and mercy' to human beings.
     That is the simplest opposition in the passage. But to get to it, you might feel that you have to work your way through some very complex and confusing images. Our natural instinct is to want to make sense of Satan as we might do with a character in a novel. We are likely to think of him as a human figure, but the *actual* descriptions in this paragraph prevent us from seeing him entirely in this way; a series of images and similes – and the idea of the simile is something that is very important in *Paradise Lost* – deny the simple idea of his resemblance to any human figure. He is repeatedly compared to beasts and monsters. There is, then, a second tension in the passage, between our desire to see Satan in human terms, and the actual description of him in the text.

c)   *Analyse the details of the passage, relating them to the oppositions already noted*
This second tension, between the 'good' that is human and known, and the 'evil' that is bestial and unknown partly arises because we are encouraged to humanise Satan – the passage speaks of him 'talking to his nearest mate', of his head being 'uplift above the wave'. Nothing here suggests a figure that is other than human and 'normal' in size. Suddenly, however, that comfortable picture

is contradicted: Satan has 'other parts' which are 'extended long and large', suggesting something bestial, unnatural. The tension is between a 'human' Satan who will draw our sympathy, and a huge, monstrous Satan who will stimulate our fear.

But where does this get us? We seem to have worked out something about the method Milton employs to present Satan, but how does this relate to the larger significance of the poem? What is perhaps most important to see is that some very basic issues are being explored. The poem is written by a poet attempting to understand and justify God's ways. There is a huge gap between the human and the divine: we, with our limited understanding, try to hang on to human figures, we try to make things understandable and explicable in human terms, but the alienating descriptions of Satan leave us confused, trying to understand huge, baffling issues. Just as we ponder God's intentions for the world, the poem also forces us to consider the place of human beings in God's scheme of things. What are people like? How much faith can we place in human resourcefulness and human independence?

These questions are also at the centre of the other opposition in the passage, the opposition between the will of Satan and the will of God. This central conflict poses two questions. First, how can created beings have 'free will' if they are ruled by an all-knowing God? And, second, if God is all-powerful, how and why does He allow evil to flourish? The tension is obvious in the closing lines of the passage. Satan's 'purpose' clearly lies beyond his own narrow ambitions. Left to his own devices he seeks only to do 'evil to others'. The result of his endeavours, however, is to 'bring forth/Infinite goodness, grace and mercy' for Man, while further damaging his own position. The simple opposition between good and evil is made more complex: no matter what dark deeds he attempts, the end result will benefit Man and further damage Satan. This paradox is something to consider throughout *Paradise Lost* if we are to get the measure of the poem. But for the moment I need to take stock, and then, in step (e), tie up some loose ends with this particular passage.

d)   *Try to say how the passage relates to the Book as a whole*
I think that we can start to see how Satan might prove a fascinating figure for the reader. All right, we may say to ourselves, so Satan is ultimately doomed to failure, but it is going to be interesting

watching what he does on the way. Milton is fully conscious of
the human desire to sympathise with the *endeavours* of a character,
while standing aside from that character's faults. It is not too
hard to see how the tensions and conflicts that Milton creates
around Satan involve us in the poem's pattern of good and evil
and engage us with its evil figure. Quite simply, we might know
that God is good and that Satan is evil, but God is a rather
remote figure, whereas Satan here has ordinary human failings –
of ambition, etc. – and so we might find ourselves, to a certain
extent, sympathising with him.

e) *Search for anything distinctive about the passage, particularly in the
    area of style, which you have not already noted*
A lot of the images, however, present a thoroughly unpleasant
image of Satan. Notice how Milton multiplies the images in order
to hammer home his point. He does not simply write 'Satan was
as big as a giant', but names three or four giants from mythology,
consistently repeating 'or' in order to make his point. Finally, as
the culmination of his images, he settles on the whale, which he
calls 'Leviathan', in the little tale of sailors anchoring their boat on
a whale in the confusion of darkness. This, however, strengthens
the opposition between good and evil in a very subtle way. In
metaphorical terms it is we humans who, in the 'confusion' of
the darkness of this world, are prone to 'anchor' ourselves upon
what appears to be a safe refuge, but which is in fact completely the
opposite. Milton's 'comfortable little story' captures the tension
that lies at the heart of his characterisation of Satan. We should
not be deceived by Satan, we should see through him, we should
see him for the evil character he is.

   Satan, then, it is becoming clear, is a central part of the conflict
between good and evil in the text. But what about the other
'characters'? Let us examine a slightly shorter passage describing
these to see if the ideas that are beginning to emerge will still
hold true.

4   *Select a third passage for discussion*

Moving on through the material in Book I, we come to paragraph
13 which follows immediately upon Satan's 'rallying call' to his
companions:

Forthwith, from every squadron and each band,
The heads and leaders thither haste where stood
Their great commander; godlike shapes and forms
Excelling human, princely dignities,
And powers that erst in heaven sat on thrones;
Though of their names in heav'nly records now
Be no memorial, blotted out and razed
By their rebellion from the Books of Life.
Nor had they yet among the sons of Eve
Got them new names, till wand'ring o'er the earth,
Through God's high sufferance for the trial of man,
By falsities and lies the greatest part
Of mankind they corrupted to forsake
God their Creator, and th' invisible
Glory of him that made them to transform
Oft to the image of a brute, adorned
With gay religions full of pomp and gold,
And devils to adore for deities:
Then were they known to men by various names,
And various idols through the heathen world.
                                    (Book I, ll. 356–75)

I shall repeat the stages that we used in examining the previous
passage in order to reinforce my method.

a)   *Make a short statement of what the passage is about*
The fallen angels are described as they rise up from the burning
lake in Hell after Satan has addressed them. This passage is similar
to the previous one in that we are given a group of figures who
seem to be 'human' rather than 'angelic'.

b)   *Search for an opposition or tension within the passage*
The opposition here is between the forces of evil, initially attractive
and appealing but in the long term destructive, and the forces of
good, often less immediately sympathetic but ultimately to our
benefit.

c)   *Analyse the details of the passage, relating them to the opposition
     already noted*
The description of the fallen angels appears to be fairly 'positive'
in tone. But then we read that as far as Heaven is concerned,

these figures no longer exist, their names have been 'rased/By their rebellion'. The effect of this creates a momentary sympathy on the reader's part followed by its immediate removal. These creatures will become the gods and idols of the pagan world, but for the time being they are practically non-existent. There is a similar opposition in the references to the deeds that they will perform, which will corrupt 'the greatest part/Of Mankind', so that they will worship these 'devils' as false 'deities'. This stresses man's willingness to follow things of a surface value rather than cling to the more difficult truth which is an 'invisible Glory'. I don't think there is much more to be said about the details of the passage, although there are some interesting points about the language and imagery, which I will look at later.

d) *Try to say how the passage relates to the Book as a whole*
We have established two or three points that are adding to our critical picture of Book I. This is a poem that deals full square with the major opposition between good and evil. The passages we have examined have shown a number of points of tension. Central to these has been the character of Satan, who clearly dominates the text. The poem is somewhat ambiguous in its approach to Satan and his fallen angels, although it is careful to stress their more obvious 'evil' characteristics. They are all criminals and rebels, and Satan is a military commander of an army of rebels. Our interest in them springs largely from the ambiguity of their presentation – Satan is, despite his evil ways, an attractive figure.

Let us consider the broader implications of this. In Christian terms – and Milton was a Christian – we are 'fallen' human beings. What I mean by this is that, after Eve's temptation in the Garden in Eden, we all lost our original innocence, and live in a corrupt world, where evil exists. Just as Eve was tempted, so we are likely to be tempted – we might well be 'seduced' by the superficially attractive qualities of a figure such as Satan. Satan is full of pride, and we, as inhabitants of a fallen world, are also full of pride. We no longer quietly and passively accept our place in God's scheme of things. These are some of the issues the poem is exploring: where and how we fit into God's scheme for the world. The poem, to a certain extent, encourages us to sympathise with Satan, as this is a way of endorsing the idea of our human limitations: we might enjoy the energy, the vitality of Satan over and above God's austere regime, even though God's plan for the world is the important thing in the long run. So, the poem's consideration of good and evil is always forcing us to consider how the world as a whole, and the people in it, accept or relate to ideas of God's authority and ideas of independence and human rebelliousness.

e)   *Search for anything distinctive about the passage, particularly in the area of style, which you have not already noted*

There is always a complication in Milton's descriptions: we always see the rottenness behind what is initially impressive. The vocabulary applied to Satan and his fallen angels is thus very interesting. The angels are initially described as 'heads and leaders' of 'squadrons' and 'bands' going to meet their 'great Commander'. The previous passages we examined stressed Satan's criminal and bestial nature. Here the stress is upon his military nature and that of his forces, suggesting that they are well-ordered and impressive. The appealing nature of the angels is recorded in a vocabulary that reminds the reader of royalty – 'princely', 'godlike', 'powers', 'thrones'. These words, however, take on a subtle tension of their own when they are set in the context of the date of composition of *Paradise Lost*. Milton was writing shortly after the restoration of the monarchy in England which followed a period of some eleven years when the country was a 'republic' without a king. In 1649 Parliament had executed Charles I on a charge of high treason, a deed that Milton very much supported since he was basically anti-royalist. (See my Chapter 3 for more details on this historical context.) A phrase such as 'princely dignities', therefore, which initially sounds impressive, can also convey the emptiness and pride of human aspirations.

Similarly, when the text describes the fallen angels as becoming heathen deities, it is in the context of 'gay religions full of pomp and gold', which stresses the *irony* of these 'materialist' religious beliefs. Irony is a most important element of Milton's style, because it allows him to suggest things that he may not have been able to say outright. The ironic use of language associated with areas of society which are normally considered worthy of praise – royalty, the army – is a further part of the interest in reading this poem. The text attacks militarist and royalist values by using their vocabulary to describe clearly evil figures. The language itself, then, produces a tension of its own which we must be aware of as we read.

5   *Select a fourth passage for discussion*

So far we have only looked at passages containing narrative. A quick glance at the verse paragraph summary shows another major element in this Book – lines of speech. Seven of the paragraphs, a good third of the Book, consist of speeches, five of which are delivered by Satan, so obviously we need to include these in our analysis. Their importance is that they allow us to examine material which is the speaker's own, rather than the narrator's. They help us to see what Satan reveals of himself in his own words. By examining one or two of these, we can add them to what we have learned already. I shall begin at the most logical point, by exploring Satan's first speech:

> If thou beest he – but O how fall'n! how changed
> From him, who in the happy realms of light
> Clothed with transcendent brightness didst outshine
> Myriads though bright – if he whom mutual league,
> United thoughts and counsels, equal hope
> And hazard in the glorious enterprise,
> Joined with me once, now misery hath joined
> In equal ruin: into what pit thou seest
> From what highth fall'n, so much the stronger proved
> He with his thunder, and till then who knew
> The force of those dire arms? Yet not for those,
> Nor what the potent Victor in his rage
> Can else inflict, do I repent or change,
> Though changed in outward lustre, that fixed mind
> And high disdain, from sense of injured merit,
> That with the mightiest raised me to contend,
> And to the fierce contention brought along
> Innumerable forces of Spirits armed
> That durst dislike his reign, and me preferring,
> His utmost power with adverse power opposed
> In dubious battle on the plains of heav'n,
> And shook his throne. What though the field be lost?
> All is not lost; the unconquerable will,
> And study of revenge, immortal hate,
> And courage never to submit or yield:
> And what is else not to be overcome?

That glory never shall his wrath or might
Extort from me. To bow and sue for grace
With suppliant knee, and deify his power
Who from the terror of this arm so late
Doubted his empire, that were low indeed,
That were an ignominy and shame beneath
This downfall; since by fate the strength of gods
And this empyreal substance cannot fail,
Since through experience of this great event,
In arms not worse, in foresight much advanced,
We may with more successful hope resolve
To wage by force or guile eternal war
Irreconcilable to our grand Foe,
Who now triumphs, and in th' excess of joy
Sole reigning holds the tyranny of heav'n.

(Book I, ll. 84–124)

This is the longest passage we have looked at so far, but I have deliberately chosen the *whole* speech, because it is important to see this in its entirety. While reading through Satan's speech you should notice any points of conflict, tension and opposition.

a)   *Make a short statement of what the passage is about*
Satan addresses the opening part of this speech to his companion, Beelzebub, whom he has just discovered lying next to him in Hell. These lines are concerned for Beelzebub's plight, recognising his role in the recent rebellion, and placing him as the greatest of the fallen angels. The lines seem to be quiet, and to express genuine feelings for Beelzebub's suffering. Yet as soon as Satan turns to himself, around line 94, Beelzebub and his condition are rapidly forgotten. Satan's ego explodes and the speech becomes more and more an expression of self-glorification and self-justification.

b)   *Search for an opposition or tension within the passage*
The tension in Satan's speech between an awareness of others and an awareness of self reflects the central opposition between good and evil. The passage stresses the fact that Satan is in deep conflict with himself. He claims that it is his enemy, God, who holds 'the tyranny of Heaven', when we can see that he himself is the tyrant of the piece, dragging his forces even deeper into the mire he

has created, rather than being ready to admit defeat and sue for mercy. A further tension relates to the lingering doubt as to the 'right' of Satan's position. Clearly, God cannot be a tyrant, yet the passage engages with the difficulty in judging whether a ruling figure is or is not tyrannical.

c)   *Analyse the details of the passage, relating them to the oppositions already noted*

Satan's words move rapidly from recognition of his situation and how much has been lost, through a simple sense of self-pity to a rousing defiance of God and a rejection of the defeat he has suffered. Within these forty lines, Satan acknowledges God's power – 'so much the stronger proved/He with his thunder' – reiterates his own right to challenge that power – 'That with the Mightiest raised me to contend' – and resolves to continue 'To wage by force or guile eternal war'. We also see for the first time Satan's *pride*. He refuses to submit to God's will, to seek forgiveness for having rebelled against him. Satan refuses to accept defeat because he believes that he was, and is, right to reject God. God defeated him, he believes, because of a superior force of arms rather than by proving that the *cause* was wrong. Our response to the Satan revealed in this speech is that we are both shocked and appalled at his inability to perceive that God's authority is unquestionable and yet we are reluctant admirers of his fortitude and resolution. Satan, then, is clearly depicted as being evil – he is an arrogant, proud, vain creature, tyrannical and uncaring in his quest for power. Yet he also appears to have elements of good about him, for he can reveal aspects of his character which are selfless and apparently caring.

d)   *Try to say how the passage relates to the Book as a whole*

The main thing we have learned from this passage is about the central role of Satan in the conflict between good and evil. We have discovered that he represents evil in this conflict, but the text also seems to be suggesting that the tension between these two forces may be seen more subtly. There is actually a conflict *within* the character of Satan, who seems to have the potential for thoughts that the reader associates with goodness. These are quickly scotched, but their presence adds to the depth of characterisation and increases our interest in the poem. Satan, it is suggested, is an alienated figure deserving of his justifiable punishment – the problems lie in the reader's understanding and acceptance of these very words: 'alienated', 'deserving', 'justifiable'. These all create a degree of sympathy that contradicts our knowledge of Satan as evil.

e)   *Search for anything distinctive about the passage, particularly in the area of style, which you have not already noted*
Once again the tensions of the subject matter are reinforced and supported by the tensions present in the language and structure. Satan's words balance between resignation and resolve, between selflessness and selfishness. The main point of balance occurs almost exactly half way through the piece with the question 'What though the field be lost?' Before this, there had been some hope that Satan might be recognising his failure and accepting his defeat. After it, this becomes impossible as his words drive towards the inevitable conclusion. Notice, also, how Milton frequently doubles up on words or phrases in order to reinforce the material, and how often phrases including 'and' or 'or' occur – 'thoughts *or* counsels', 'hope *and* hazard', 'repent, *or* change', 'fixed mind, / *And* high disdain'.
   The most significant structural device in this speech, however, is the use of a technique known as 'dramatic tension'. We would normally expect to find this device used in plays, but a piece of poetry that is written as a speech is just as likely to use it. Milton is particularly good at writing dramatic speeches because he is clearly aware of the use that can be made of dramatic tension in holding the attention of the 'audience', and in manipulating the audience's response to the character who is speaking. Many elements go to the making of successful dramatic tension, and all the playwright's devices may be found in this passage: repetition, change of pace, change of mood, surging to a climax, then falling back, and, throughout the speech, building up a confidence and mastery of the material through a careful control of phrasing and syntax. Dramatic tension underpins the whole of Satan's speech, transforming it into a powerful piece of dramatic poetry that is as effective as any Shakespearean soliloquy. Let us look, briefly, at how we may see two or three of these effects in action.
   First, change of pace and repetition. Just after the pivotal sentence I mentioned, 'What though the field be lost?', there occurs

Satan's statement of the reasons for his continuing with his rebellion. The sentence begins with a simple, definite statement: 'All is
not lost'; this is then followed by phrases that are studded (both
visually when you look at them, and aurally when you read them or
hear them) with the word 'And', a repetitive device which creates
a series of hammer-blow convictions. After this sentence there is a
very short phrase, merely a line and a half: 'That were an ignominy
and shame beneath / This downfall'. So, the pace changes rapidly
from short, to long and repetitive, to short again.

Second, there is the use of the surge to a climax. The closing
sentence contains fifteen and a half lines of rising fury in which
the tension is raised by means of pauses as well as by vocabulary.
Satan's venom is initially constrained by short phrases marked by
semi-colons, but then is finally unleashed after the crucial word
'Since'. In a sentence which almost exists as separate from the
main sentence, we find phrasing that is complex and yet still highly
articulate. Dramatic tension is present here in the conflict between
the difficulty of the phrasing and the simplicity of the meaning
which is that Satan is grandly stating that they can hope to win
another war. The use of dramatic tension helps a great deal in
enhancing our understanding and appreciation of this passage of
speech.

I think we need here to examine a further speech by Satan to
ensure that our interpretation is on the right tracks. Of course,
you can select any number of passages to examine, and normally
in this book I will be taking just four passages per chapter. Here,
however, because it may be helpful, I am going to select an extra
passage at this stage. I have chosen another complete speech,
Satan's fourth, paragraph 12 of the summary, although this is
much shorter than the previous one. The reason for choosing
this speech is that it shows Satan speaking to a much more general
audience, and therefore reveals a bolder, more 'public' side of the
characterisation:

> Princes, Potentates,
> Warriors, the flow'r of heav'n, once yours, now lost,
> If such astonishment as this can seize
> Eternal Spirits; or have ye chos'n this place
> After the toil of battle to repose
> Your wearied virtue, for the ease you find

To slumber here, as in the vales of heav'n?
Or in this abject posture have ye sworn
To adore the Conqueror, who now beholds
Cherub and Seraph rolling in the flood
With scattered arms and ensigns, till anon
His swift pursuers from heav'n gates discern
Th' advantage, and descending tread us down
Thus drooping, or with linked thunderbolts
Transfix us to the bottom of this gulf?
Awake, arise, or be for ever fall'n!

(Book I, ll. 315–30)

a)   *Make a short statement of what the passage is about*
On this occasion Satan is addressing all the fallen angels, calling
upon them to stir themselves from their stupor of defeat in the
'oceans' of Hell.

b)   *Search for an opposition or tension within the passage*
The passage reinforces our vision of Satan as a force for destruction; it maintains the tension between good and evil by allowing us
to have a niggling respect for the persistence he shows in the face
of hopeless odds. There may not be the direct opposition that we
saw in the previous example, but there remains the tension which
arises from the increasingly subtle characterisation of Satan.

c)   *Analyse the details of the passage, relating them to the opposition
      already noted*
There is no note of *praise* for the fallen angels in this speech –
they are addressed in heavily ironic terms which suggest idleness
and sloth rather than valour. To Satan these are tired, defeated
creatures, taking up an 'abject posture', ready to admit the superiority of God. He rails against them for this, striking a note of terror
by suggesting that the forces of God may even now pursue them
in order to inflict further punishment. The irony present here
indicates Satan's ambiguity. He needs the support of the fallen
angels, yet he can only assure them by being *offensive* to them.
He offers them nothing, no hope, no expectations, merely the
threat of greater punishment to come. The irony underlying the
speech reinforces the central tension – all Satan *can* offer them
is further punishment. More and greater evil, if you like. He has,

however, convinced himself that it is worth continuing the fight. That persistence becomes the means by which he is able to rouse his troops, and we are stirred by it. The tension is once again there in this conflict between failure and conviction on Satan's part, and between admiration and contempt on ours.

d)   *Try to say how the passage relates to the Book as a whole*
The passage seems to confirm the pattern we have been tracing. The central conflict between good and evil is present in the portrayal of Satan, with which we tend to feel immediate revulsion but also a degree of sympathy, as we watch a figure who carries on in the face of apparently overwhelming odds.

e)   *Search for anything distinctive about the passage, particularly in the area of style, which you have not already noted*
The ambiguous nature of Satan's position is strongly indicated in the opening few lines, known in rhetorical terms as an 'apostrophe'. Once again, a militaristic and royalist vocabulary is used of the fallen angels – 'Princes, potentates, warriors' – terms which, as we have seen, indicate something bad. These are then followed by the phrase 'the flower of Heaven' which appears, at first, to be continuing the list of attributes. Yet the next phrase reveals otherwise – these angels are not the 'flower of Heaven', for that is what they have *lost*, although Satan's immediate 'if' suggests that this may not be a permanent loss. Satan's description of the angels' situation is even more ironic in the light of the names that he uses to speak to them. These figures, represented by words reserved for monarchs and soldiers, are now vanquished and crushed, and their leader can only arouse them by heaping scorn and abuse on their heads. Again, the speech is high in dramatic tension, its scornful phrasing with the repeated *or*s, as well as the sense breaking over lines in a movement that disrupts the order of the verse, matching the tone of the subject matter.

6   *Have I achieved a sufficiently complex sense of the text?*

We have begun to see how the text manipulates the reader's interest in character in order to highlight the central opposition between good and evil. This is presented in just sufficiently complex a way as to maintain a constant sense of ambiguity in our response to the text, as well as in our understanding of that response. We have begun to arrive at a critical response to the subject matter principally by means of the characterisation, in particular the figure of Satan. There is a definite *consistency* in this Book of *Paradise Lost* which emerges in the ways in which the material, through the presentation of an idea or a figure, constantly refers to the central opposition between good and evil. We are also beginning to see how the language and structure of the Book supports and reinforces this.

The central thrust of our method of study has been to examine the tension that exists between good and evil in Book I of *Paradise Lost*. What I think we have learned is that these two words do, indeed, offer a source of tension and conflict in revealing the doubt and ambiguity that exist in the description of, as well as 'within', the character of Satan. Evil set against good is a primary opposition, and our examination of the passages selected has shown that this opposition occurs at all points in the text. The importance of the good/evil opposition needs to be further explored as it is one of the central aspects of the whole of *Paradise Lost*.

What, though, can we say to conclude our examination of Book I? It is without doubt filled with tensions and conflicts which arise from one central opposition. These include ideas such as leadership, rebellion, authority and stability in political terms; courage, weakness, valour, strength, pride in personal terms. As an 'opening chapter', Book I indicates many points of interest, but shows that Satan is used as the central figure in the exploration of complex issues. There are many aspects I have not touched upon, of course, but you may return to these in the future. For now, let us move on into Book II in order to show how the method can be applied there, and in order to deepen our understanding of the whole poem. Although there will be questions that remain unanswered, the method introduced in this chapter has begun to show one way of how to deal with what is a dense poetic text, and how to arrive at a clear set of critical ideas which you can then take on by analyzing further passages.

2
Paradise Lost, Book II

I Constructing an overall analysis

One of the problems of studying just a single Book of *Paradise Lost* is not knowing whether to treat it as a separate unit or as part of a larger whole. What I have suggested you do is, first, try to see each Book as a 'chapter', that is try to see it as part of an unfolding pattern of ideas and tensions rather than as a complete text in itself. In that way you will, I think, remain open to the range of Milton's techniques. You will see how the poem looks forwards and backwards, and how it expects the reader to take part in what is a large drama on both the cosmic and the human scale. Second, you need to keep in mind what you have learned from looking at Book I where we discovered that a major key to unlocking the poem was the constant presence of the conflict between good and evil. This was shown to a large extent through the figure of Satan, who represents evil in his conflict with God. We saw also, though, some of the subtleties of how Milton presents this figure in that there was evidence of the good / evil conflict existing *within* Satan himself. Exploration of Book II, therefore, will give us an opportunity to examine further these aspects of the text. However, we should also try to become more aware of the complexity of the poem by widening the scope slightly. It is important to keep in mind the huge scale of the whole of *Paradise Lost*, and restricting ourselves too much to one opposition might narrow the focus. A poem as vast as this can present other potential sources of opposition. We must now start to look for two further oppositions – that between negative and positive, and that between order and chaos.

You may have noticed the order / chaos opposition in your reading of Book I. When Satan has roused the fallen angels from their stupor they move to the 'land' and build Pandemonium.

This is a form of constructing order out of chaos. The opposition between negative and positive appears in the contrast between the fallen angels' initial behaviour and their later assistance in the building of the palace. The text, then, is built out of these further oppositions which offer us keys to a deeper understanding of Book II where we shall be looking for evidence that the three major oppositions – good versus evil, order versus chaos, and negative versus positive – are present.

1   *After reading the text, think about the story and what kind of pattern you can see in it*

At this stage in Book I, I gave you two possible ways of constructing a 'summary' of its contents. The first was to use Milton's own summary as it appears in The Argument prefaced to each Book. I would prefer you to use the second method, which arises from your own reading. This is to summarise *briefly* each verse paragraph in the Book. Before you do this, read right through the Book, fairly quickly, in order to grasp some idea of the basic content and see something of the way that it is shaped. After that, construct your paragraph summary. This is mine:

1. In Pandemonium, Satan sits on a throne and addresses the fallen angels.
2. Satan's first speech. He tells them that they are all equal in Hell, since there is nothing to fight for. He asks for suggestions as to how they may regain their position in Heaven.
3. Moloch is introduced.
4. Moloch proposes an outright assault on Heaven, arguing that they have nothing to lose in so doing, because, if they were to be beaten, there could be no worse punishment than Hell, and that total destruction may in fact be preferable to an eternity in Hell.
5. Belial is introduced.
6. Belial rejects Moloch's suggestion on the grounds that God cannot be beaten, and that He will not destroy them, but *could* make their situation worse. He proposes that they

do nothing but sit and wait. God might forgive them in time, or some chance event, unforeseen, might release them.

7.   A brief narrative summary of this, then Mammon speaks.

8.   Mammon also rejects war, but on the grounds that it would be futile, and may in fact lead to the fallen angels suing for peace from God – the result of which would be humiliating. He suggests that they make the most of their present situation, perhaps turning Hell to their own advantage, but most of all imposing *order* upon their existence.

9.   The fallen angels applaud Mammon; Beelzebub is introduced.

10.   Beelzebub argues that there is no point in considering either war against Heaven or an attempt to build an equivalent empire in Hell, because God will always be the supreme being. He suggests instead that they turn their minds to Earth and its inhabitants, who may be open to defeat or deception by the fallen angels. Success here could anger God more than direct confrontation with Him.

      (A brief narrative interruption reveals that the fallen angels are much taken with this proposal, originally suggested by Satan.)

11.   Beelzebub continues by repeating his idea and calling for a champion to seek out the new world.

12.   The angels consider Beelzebub's proposals. Only Satan responds.

13.   Satan accepts the challenge, assuming the role of monarch in order that he may justify his decision. The angels rise up and praise Satan.

14.   The consultations ended, the angels leave. Narrative comment on comparison between these and men who cannot come to agreement.

15.   The angels proceed out of Pandemonium, messengers are sent to tell of their proceedings throughout Hell; they disperse to a variety of places to await Satan's return. The ways in which they occupy themselves are described in great detail. Some explore Hell, discovering all its horrors.

16.   Satan's journey to the gates of Hell. His first meeting with Sin and Death.

17.   Satan asks Death who he is.

18.   Death responds, without revealing his name, telling Satan that *he* is the ruler of Hell.

19.   Death and Satan square up to each other, ready to fight.

20.   Sin intervenes between them, revealing that they are father and son.

21.   Brief narrative link to the next paragraph.

22.   Satan asks Sin who she is, and what she means by the father/son references.

23.   Sin replies. She reveals to Satan that she sprang out of his head when he first conspired against God, was named 'Sin' by the angels in Heaven, many of whom found her attractive, particularly Satan who impregnated her. After the battle in Heaven she fell to Hell with the fallen angels and was given the key to the gates of Hell. Soon she gave birth to Death, who pursued and raped her, giving rise to the hellhounds who surround her. The only reason Death does not devour her is that he knows it will bring about his own end. The only one who can resist Death is God.

24.   Satan responds, changing his tack, telling Sin that he is venturing out of Hell alone in order to set free the fallen hosts.

25.   Narrative link indicating Sin and Death are taken in by Satan's argument.

26.   Sin responds that although forbidden to do so by God, she will open the gates of Hell for Satan.

27.   The gates of Hell are opened, but Sin is unable to close them again. They look out into the Abyss, a place where Night, Chaos and Chance are continually at war. Satan launches himself into this, buoyed on hot air currents issuing from Hell. After a terrifying journey, he reaches the pavilion where Night and Chaos sit enthroned amongst their followers.

28.   Satan addresses these, telling them that he is looking for the path to Heaven. He asks for directions, offering them the possibility of ruling in Heaven if he succeeds.

29.   Chaos replies, saying that he recognises Satan and saw all that has happened, and revealing the existence of Earth, 'linked in a golden chain' to Heaven. He speeds Satan on his way.

30.   Satan continues his journey. It is revealed that Sin and

Death are following him, building a 'bridge of monstrous length' between Hell and Earth, across which the spirits of Hell can easily pass to and fro.

31. Satan reaches the boundaries of Chaos and Nature. He sees the Earth hanging beneath Heaven and heads for it.

Book II is rather longer than Book I. While this summary is all right, it is very long, and does not really give me a version of the events which I can easily handle. So, after listing the events, you may find it helpful to pull them together into a more condensed summary, rather like Milton's Argument. This is my summary of Book II:

A council of the fallen angels is held in Pandemonium. Four of the more senior figures propose various ways of escaping from their current situation in order to revenge themselves upon God. Beelzebub's proposal to send someone to see if anything can be done with the newly-created Earth is accepted and Satan takes on the task. After a short description of life in Hell, Satan begins his journey. Having met Sin and Death, who are revealed as his 'offspring', he crosses the Abyss outside Hell and encounters Night and Chaos. When he reaches the edge of the Abyss, he sees Earth suspended beneath Heaven and makes his way towards it.

This brief summary has provided me with a manageable impression of the text. The dominant figure is again Satan. Clearly the Book has two parts – the debate in Pandemonium and Satan's journey out of Hell. This may appear to be an obvious statement, but it is worth making, because it adds to our growing sense of patterning in the text. We can also see how much this is an 'open' structure – in other words, this is an episode in a longer sequence, not a 'closed' event to be seen as separate from the other Books of *Paradise Lost*. The debate in the first part results from the construction of Pandemonium in Book I; Satan has only *seen* Earth at the end of Book II, he has not arrived there.

Another pattern which becomes clear from this summary is the continuation of the idea of opposition. The first two Books of *Paradise Lost* are concerned principally with Satan and his exploits after his expulsion from Heaven. Before Satan's rebellion the universe was harmonious, peaceful and ordered. Afterwards, all was disharmony, war and chaos. Book II, as the summary indicates, fills out our picture of that disruption in the terrifying figures of Death and Sin as well as through Night and Chaos. Again, the tensions which underlie this conflict are stressed by means of ambiguity. The second part of the Book, by stressing the anarchy of the Abyss, reflects the sense in which even Hell is an ordered state of some kind. Initially, at least, the gates of Hell are closed against the outside, which not only kept its inhabitants in, but also kept the far worse forces out. Satan deliberately and contemptuously disrupts even this order. Dissatisfied with his position in Heaven, he rebelled against the jurisdiction of God. Failing, inevitably, in this task, he is punished by expulsion to Hell where his dissatisfaction continues and leads to his disturbing the far more frightening forces of a universe that will forever be in conflict as a result. God alone is capable of sustaining the barriers of order and quelling the forces of Chaos, but Satan refuses to acknowledge this fact and unleashes further anarchy. Unless the forces of evil are repelled, everything will disintegrate into the inconceivable ruin of Chaos and anarchy.

The debate in the first part of the Book stresses the opposition between negative and positive. An initial response to these speeches is that the leaders of the fallen angels are making positive moves to improve their situation. Much of what is said, however, is negative, each speaker only emphasising his own way of seeing things. The result is that each speaker opposes or contradicts the previous one, giving no sense of rational discussion. All four speakers submit proposals which pursue their own selfish ideas. Moloch is a warmonger, Belial is slothful, Mammon is materialistic, and Beelzebub, while proposing a highly dangerous solution, is careful not to volunteer himself for the task. These speakers are negative because they do not care about the fate of their companions. In the second part of the Book Satan is constantly in conflict with those he encounters. This is heightened by his assumption of the ruling position in Hell, which is negative when we remember that he initially stressed the 'equality' supposed to exist among the fallen angels.

These, then, are the basic ideas about the key oppositions which I can gather from Book II. Now we need to move to a closer examination of the text itself, bearing these points in mind as we go. Let us go on to Step 2.

2 *Select a short passage for discussion and try to build on the ideas you have established so far*

When selecting passages it is often best to look for one which you found particularly memorable when you first read the Book. Alternatively, you might choose one that you feel you can make good progress with. The first one you look at should be a fairly easy one to analyse. You should not be afraid of starting at an easy point, because it gives you confidence in handling the material. There is no real reason why these ones should be chosen 'chronologically', and in fact my first passage is paragraph 27 of the summary, which occurs nearer the end of the Book:

> She opened, but to shut
> Excelled her power; the gates wide open stood,
> That with extended wings a bannered host
> Under spread ensigns marching might pass through
> With horse and chariots ranked in loose array;
> So wide they stood, and like a furnace mouth
> Cast forth redounding smoke and ruddy flame.
> Before their eyes in sudden view appear
> The secrets of the hoary deep, a dark
> Illimitable ocean without bound,
> Without dimension; where length, breadth, and highth,
> And time and place are lost; where eldest Night
> And Chaos, ancestors of Nature, hold
> Eternal anarchy, amidst the noise
> Of endless wars, and by confusion stand.
> For Hot, Cold, Moist, and Dry, four champions fierce,
> Strive here for mast'ry, and to battle bring
> Their embryon atoms; they around the flag
> Of each his faction, in their several clans,
> Light-armed or heavy, sharp, smooth, swift or slow,
> Swarm populous, unnumbered as the sands
> Of Barca or Cyrene's torrid soil,
> Levied to side with warring winds, and poise
> Their lighter wings.
>   (Book II, ll. 883–906)

This is a relatively short passage and, as in the previous chapter,

I shall look for the oppositions we have identified as reflecting the tensions evident in the whole poem. Again I shall use the stages of analysis I gave you in the previous chapter in order to clarify the method.

a)   *Make a short statement of what the passage is about*
This passage presents the opening of the gates of Hell by Sin, and gives a description of the Abyss which exists outside together with the various elements which exist there, as it is seen by Sin, Death and Satan.

b)   *Search for an opposition or tension within the passage*
The central opposition in this passage is between order and chaos. Satan peers out from the gateway of Hell into a place which is so indescribably disordered that it makes Hell itself seem a comforting refuge. Everything in the Abyss is in conflict, from the huge 'eternal anarchy' of Night and Chaos, to the minute battle of the 'embryon atoms'. The opposition of order and chaos is further reflected in the tension that exists in the text itself as it attempts to impose a literary structure, or order, upon the incomprehensible abstract concept that Chaos represents.

c)   *Analyse the details of the passage, relating them to the opposition already noted*
The first six and a half lines present the gates of Hell themselves – their size, what issues or could issue from them, how they can never be closed again once opened. The text clings to the order that the gates represent, no matter how horrible their aspect. Beyond lies genuine chaos, a huge chasm of nothing against which even Satan rebels in fear and loathing. The language of order is irrelevant here, for all five of the dimensions we normally associate with space and time are 'lost'. The tension which results from this is partly contained when Night, Chaos, and Nature are turned into 'characters' in this drama, together with what were, for the seventeenth century, the four *elements* of the natural world – Hot, Cold, Moist and Dry. Harmony and balance between these elements should represent genuine order but in the Abyss they are forces of conflict. Yet words almost fail to convey the image. The text seems to search for adequate metaphors, ending with the rather unsatisfactory 'unnumbered as the sands / Of Barca

or Cyrene's torrid soil' – a desert image for an arid vocabulary. Nevertheless, the text finally does present the sheer terror of absolute chaos. The Abyss is the physical image of negative forces, all of which will be unleashed by Satan's desire to take revenge on God. All life, whether mortal or immortal, needs order, for without it there is chaos, and chaos is nothing, which literally means no thing, something truly beyond comprehension. This passage, we might argue, reveals the author engaging with the impossible and, while acknowledging the futility of the task, imposing a sense of order that makes the impossible *manageable*.

d)   *Try to say how the passage relates to the Book as a whole*
The passage reflects the concern of Book II with the opposition between order and chaos. It also develops the characterisation of Satan. Although Satan is the figure of evil, there are forces worse than he is, against which he appears to be more than a cardboard cut-out figure. One of the subtleties of the whole poem, then, is the way in which Satan is shown to be a very plausible figure, because otherwise we might reject him as the source of all mankind's subsequent problems. One other point of interest here is the way in which the passage uses the natural order of things, such as the five dimensions, or the four elements. Satan journeys to Earth in order to disrupt the harmony and order of God's creation, aided by the unnatural and chaotic forces of the Abyss.

e)   *Search for anything distinctive about the passage, particularly in the area of style, which you have not already noted*
The passage uses military language, as before, to describe the forces of evil, as well as the occupants of the Abyss. The gates of Hell are wide enough for a large army, images of which are drawn from a mixture of medieval and Biblical sources. The four elements are described as 'four champions fierce', around the flags of which the 'embryon atoms' are to be found 'in their several clans'. For Milton, clearly, war is a hateful concept. Also note the emphasis placed upon items of military equipment which are normally associated with the more 'praiseworthy' aspects of an army – the flags, banners and ensigns. Here they suggest the pride and folly of war and destruction, rather than any idea of 'national pride' which is one of the principal devices used by Satan

in his attempts to convince his allies of the values of following his course of action.

There may be other features of the text here that interest you. What is important is that you try to relate those details to your larger sense of the poem, so that you build up your own analysis. My analysis is clearly leading me to look more and more at war images and chaos. To develop and also to check my ideas, I need to go on to another passage.

3   Select a second passage for discussion

For my second passage I want to look at a further piece of the narrative material rather than at one of the speeches dominating the first part of Book II. Obviously I will have to look at a speech, but for the moment I want to concentrate on the narrative and its impact. These lines, paragraph 14 of the summary, occur immediately after the close of the opening 'debate':

> Thus they their doubtful consultations dark
> Ended rejoicing in their matchless Chief:
> As when from mountain tops the dusky clouds
> Ascending, while the north wind sleeps, o'erspread
> Heav'n's cheerful face, the louring element
> Scowls o'er the darkened landscape snow or show'r;
> If chance the radiant sun with farewell sweet
> Extend his ev'ning beam, the fields revive,
> The birds their notes renew, and bleating herds
> Attest their joy, that hill and valley rings.
> O shame to men! Devil with devil damned
> Firm concord holds, men only disagree
> Of creatures rational, though under hope
> Of heavenly grace; and, God proclaiming peace,
> Yet live in hatred, enmity, and strife
> Among themselves, and levy cruel wars,
> Wasting the earth, each other to destroy:
> As if (which might induce us to accord)
> Man had not hellish foes enow besides,
> That day and night for his destruction wait.
>
> (Book II, ll. 486–505)

a)   *Make a short statement of what the passage is about*
The fallen angels rejoice after the debate in Pandemonium. Their
feelings are indicated by means of a simile describing sunlight
falling on a wintry scene. The agreement they have reached is
contrasted with the apparent inability of Man ever to agree.

b)   *Search for an opposition or tension within the passage*
Central to this passage is the opposition between the apparently
positive outcome of the fallen angels' debate and the negative
ways in which men try to resolve their differences. The opposition
is particularly shown in terms of war and peace, because the
angels have achieved peace or 'concord' by means of their debate,
whereas men are always at war because of their disagreements.

c)   *Analyse the details of the passage, relating them to the opposition
      already noted*
The simile which opens this passage presents a dark and gloomy
winter landscape momentarily pierced by a beam of sunlight. As a
result of that beam the whole of the landscape and its occupants,
bathed in light, become joyful. Initially, this simile describes the
feelings of the fallen angels now that they have agreed to the
course they must take. After the wintry aspect of their recognition
of their situation in Hell, the positive unity of purpose they have
now achieved is like a shaft of sunlight, brightening their pros-
pects. However, the simile also adds a further complication. The
angels are now at 'peace' because they have reached agreement,
but they have resolved to pursue their war against God. The
peace is false, because it is an agreement to further the cause
of destruction. In the second part of the passage the narrator
pours scorn upon men for constantly living in 'hatred, enmity
and strife/Among themselves', always resorting to 'cruel wars' in
their attempts to achieve agreement. They do this although they
are fully aware of the peace that is offered by God. It is ironic that
while peace is genuinely available to men, if they are willing to
accept it as God's gift, the fallen angels will never achieve genuine
peace since their rebellion in Heaven means that they are eternally
condemned to live in Hell. The passage ends by highlighting the
foolishness of humankind, avoiding peace in pursuit of war, while
the forces of evil, who are the real enemies, and against whom they
should strive, are uniting in opposition against them.

d)   *Try to say how the passage relates to the Book as a whole*
Book II is concerned with the development of Satan's stated aim
to continue his war against Heaven and its forces. There will be
no peace until he achieves his aims, but he will never achieve
his aims, so there will be no peace. The apparent 'peace' which
occurs here, at the heart of Book II, highlights the ambiguities of
the conflict between good and evil. The forces of evil are being
shown in positive ways, while the forces of good are revealed to be
negative. This creates a strong contrast which again involves the
reader in the poem's dramatic events and analysis.

e)   *Search for anything distinctive about the passage, particularly in the
area of style, which you have not already noted*
The simile which opens the passage is in what is called the *pastoral*
mode, that is, it deals with classical, positive elements of the natural
world, the sky, the landscape, the singing of birds and the bleating
of herds of sheep. This is in sharp contrast to the negative objects
of the simile – the fallen angels and their situation in Hell, a
place of horror and torment. When the verse turns to its scornful
accusations against humankind, the *syntax*, that is the order of the
words themselves, rises in pace to a ruinous climax, introducing
many short phrases and eventually becoming much more direct in
its statements. The language of the passage emphasises again the
conflicts and ambiguities of the content. In the opening phrase
'their doubtful consultations dark', the potential ambiguity of the
word 'doubtful' is interesting. The fallen angels are not in doubt,
for they have, they believe, resolved upon a course of action. The
doubt belongs rather with the narrator who, since he knows the
outcome of their debate, is aware of what it actually means. We see
the emptiness of the angels' schemes, how they consult and draw
up plans, but how this is only an ironic, and empty, echo of God's
order for the world. By extension, we see the vanity and emptiness
of all human pride and aspiration when set against God's larger
scheme of things. Yet we never quite lose our sympathy with
characters who attempt to build some semblance of order in a
void, even if they have been instrumental in creating that void.
It is a view of good and evil from a writer who recognises he is one
of the fallen and can, accordingly, sympathise.
    I think that I have now gained enough from this passage and I
need to move on.

4   Select a third passage for discussion

Fifteen of the thirty-one paragraphs indicated in my summary of
Book II contain speeches by a number of speakers. These vary in
length from simple questions of less than ten lines to the lengthy
passages spoken in Pandemonium, of which Beelzebub's, at almost
100 lines in total, is probably the longest. The major oppositions of
the poem can clearly be found in the narrative material, now we
need to see if this is also true of the spoken material. I intend to
begin by looking at the second part of Beelzebub's address. This
is paragraph 11 of the summary:

> Well have ye judged, well ended long debate,
> Synod of gods, and like to what ye are,
> Great things resolved; which from the lowest deep
> Will once more lift us up, in spite of fate,
> Nearer our ancient seat; perhaps in view
> Of those bright confines, whence with neighbouring arms
> And opportune excursion we may chance
> Re-enter heav'n; or else in some mild zone
> Dwell not unvisited of heav'n's fair light
> Secure, and at the bright'ning orient beam
> Purge off this gloom; the soft delicious air
> To heal the scar of these corrosive fires
> Shall breathe her balm. But first whom shall we send
> In search of this new world, whom shall we find
> Sufficient? Who shall tempt with wand'ring feet
> The dark unbottomed infinite abyss
> And through the palpable obscure find out
> His uncouth way, or spread his airy flight
> Upborne with indefatigable wings
> Over the vast abrupt, ere he arrive
> The happy isle; what strength, what art can then
> Suffice, or what evasion bear him safe
> Through the strict senteries and stations thick
> Of angels watching round? Here he had need
> All circumspection, and we now no less
> Choice in our suffrage; for on whom we send,
> The weight of all and our last hope relies.

> > (Book II, ll. 390–416)

a) *Make a short statement of what the passage is about*
Beelzebub congratulates and praises the council of fallen angels
for accepting his advice and offers glimpses of what might happen
if they are successful. He then outlines the qualities required by
the one who is to be their champion and asks who this might be.

b) *Search for an opposition or tension within the passage*
The central opposition in this passage is between the negative
aspect of doubt and the positive aspect of certainty. Beelzebub
at first is positive in his manner, convinced that his suggestion is
the best. He then becomes negative, however, because he does not
know what the salvation will be, he does not know what attributes
the champion will need, and he does not know who that champion
will be. The opposition between the positive and negative qualities
of Beelzebub's speech is also strengthened by a tension which is set
up in its structure.

c) *Analyse the details of the passage, relating them to the opposition
    already noted*
The passage opens with a tone of congratulation that is very close
to flattery, since Beelzebub is praising his colleagues for having
accepted his own proposal. At first positive and certain, a close
reading of these lines shows an underlying tension which implies
self-glorification rather than genuine delight in the agreement
of others. In fact, the narrative interruption which precedes this
section of Beelzebub's address (see the summary of paragraph 10)
suggests that his plan was actually 'devised/By Satan', which puts
forward the idea that the present speaker is only a mouthpiece of
his master. The congratulations he extends are, then, a piece of
distasteful and very negative obsequiousness.

Next we see the details of Beelzebub's vision of what will result
from the 'great things' which the angels have 'resolved'. The
course of action, he is convinced, will 'once more lift us up', but
(and once again the opposition of negative and positive enters)
it will not return them to their former glory, only bring them
'Nearer our ancient seat'. Success in this course of action must
be 'in spite of fate' which casts doubt upon the plan. Beelzebub
offers nothing more certain than that they may regain a distant
sight of Heaven, 'perhaps', and if they can find an 'opportune
excursion', they may 'chance/Re-enter Heaven'. Even that may

not be possible: in which case, Beelzebub suggests, they may find some 'mild zone' where they may securely pass their existence in a region that is 'not unvisited of heaven's fair light'. Beelzebub does not and cannot know with certainty whether his imaginings will ever come true. The whole of his plan, so positive in its apparent certainty, is riddled with doubts and uncertainties that make it hopelessly negative in reality.

Then there is the further uncertainty related to the finding of one amongst them who will go 'In search of this new world'. The qualities of this unknown character are presented by means of a series of questions, which, again, appear positive and convincing, yet almost all of which contain doubts or hesitancies. Beelzebub does not know whether this deed may be achieved through 'art' or 'evasion', and whoever should go, the burden upon his shoulders will be huge, for he will represent the angels' 'last hope'. Failure in this enterprise will reduce all of them to the totally negative state of final despair.

d)   *Try to say how the passage relates to the Book as a whole*
Beelzebub's speech closes the discussion stage of the council in Pandemonium. All that is left is Satan's acceptance of the challenge and his assumption of the role of leader. On the surface confident and forward-looking, the speech in reality is filled with doubt and uncertainty, offering an illusion of a better future, about which Beelzebub is ignorant. The rational debate of the first half of Book II is little more than a hollow exchange of words. The fallen angels will not suffer any further as a result of Beelzebub's proposal, at least not in the immediate future, and there is the remote possibility that they will in fact ultimately benefit. The angels are seen to be a group of evil, self-seeking figures concerned only about their own situations. They are willing to support a plan that does not require their personal involvement, particularly as the task will be carried out by a single volunteer, and his only motive is likely to be self-glorification.

e)   *Search for anything distinctive about the passage, particularly in the area of style, which you have not already noted*
I can't see much more to say about the style of the passage. What is important is its irony. The plan Beelzebub offers is, in fact, Satan's; it should be seen as a devious plan to boost the latter's position

again, after the failure of the war against Heaven. Beelzebub acts as a mouthpiece to fool the angels into accepting yet another of Satan's ploys to oppose God. As we have already seen over and over again, nothing is as it seems amongst the fallen angels. Everything is a deceit; what sounds impressive proves to be hollow, what looks like selflessness always proves to be selfish. This, the poem suggests, is the superficial and misleading quality of so much that we see, and tempts us, in a fallen world.

5   Select a fourth passage for discussion

The discussion of Beelzebub's speech has given me some insight into the ways in which the material in the first half of Book II sustains the central oppositions we are exploring. I want to look now at a passage from later in the Book, in order to see if a speech outside Pandemonium is similarly useful. I have chosen this next passage, paragraph 29 of the summary, as it is the last speech of Book II, addressed by Chaos to Satan:

> I know thee, stranger, who thou art,
> That mighty leading angel, who of late
> Made head against heav'n's King, though overthrown.
> I saw and heard, for such a numerous host
> Fled not in silence through the frighted deep
> With ruin upon ruin, rout on rout,
> Confusion worse confounded; and heav'n gates
> Poured out by millions her victorious bands
> Pursuing. I upon my frontiers here
> Keep residence; if all I can will serve
> That little which is left so to defend,
> Encroached on still through our intestine broils
> Weak'ning the scepter of old Night: first hell
> Your dungeon stretching far and wide beneath;
> Now lately heaven and earth, another world
> Hung o'er my realm, linked in a golden chain
> To that side heav'n from whence your legions fell.
> If that way be your walk, you have not far;
> So much the nearer danger; go and speed;
> Havoc and spoil and ruin are my gain.
>
> (Book II, ll. 990–1009)

a)   *Make a short statement of what the passage is about*
Chaos acknowledges Satan as the leader of the fallen angels,
recently defeated in the battle in Heaven. He offers his support
in defending the Abyss in order that Satan may pursue his search
for Earth.

b)   *Search for an opposition or tension within the passage*
The main opposition in this passage is between order and chaos.
The figure of Chaos wishes to support Satan's endeavours for
purely personal motives. He sees Satan's task as an opportunity
to re-establish what we might call, paradoxically, the order that
he feels is necessary in his realm. He wants to maintain a very
negative 'order' simply to allow Satan an opportunity to bring
further chaos to the created universe. Evil, negative motives are
used to bring about the destruction of the harmony and order of
God's creation.

c)   *Analyse the details of the passage, relating them to the opposition*
      already noted
The opening sentence is full of flattery. Chaos describes Satan as
'That mighty leading Angel', which indicates his opinion, and the
deflection to the end of the sentence of the knowledge that Satan
lost when he 'made head against Heaven's King' confirms this. He
also witnessed the flight of the fallen angels on their route through
the Abyss to Hell, pursued by the 'victorious bands' of Heaven.
Nevertheless, Chaos is prepared to support Satan because the
'Confusion worse confounded' of the fallen angels is very much
to his purpose. Encouragement of Satan in his destructive urges
can only be of benefit to Chaos since Satan's endeavours will
bring him gain without his actually having to involve himself. His
power is being weakened by the signs of God's ordering of the
universe, allocating space to Hell and Earth, all the while reducing
his territory to 'That little which is left'.

d)   *Try to say how the passage relates to the Book as a whole*
The passage highlights the continued presence of selfishness
amongst the figures we have so far encountered. Every figure in
this Book seeks only to further selfishness, rather than to curb it
or temper it. Equally, they are prepared to use any or all of their
'allies' in the pursuit of their desires. Chaos recognises that by

supporting Satan he will most likely gain in 'Havoc, and spoil, and ruin', which are the principles of his existence. Selfishness is a primary feature of the characterisation of Satan. By linking him with allies whose selfish motivations are as strong as his own, the text undermines any residual sympathy the reader may have for Satan. His 'heroic' endeavours have as their sole motivation self-aggrandizement or self-glorification. Satan has pronounced himself the leader of the fallen angels, and has been acknowledged as such by them and others, yet he is driven onward by his urge to revenge himself against God. The text is now exploring the nature of motive, a theme running throughout the whole of *Paradise Lost.*

e)   *Search for anything distinctive about the passage, particularly in the area of style, which you have not already noted*
This passage is very carefully structured, which indicates *dramatic tension.* There are a number of climaxes: the fleeing fallen angels, pursued by Heaven's 'victorious bands'; the description of the 'encroachment' of Hell and Earth upon the territory of Chaos; the way in which Satan is finally sent on his way. There is a frequent use of devices such as repetition and verbal patterning as in the single line, 'With ruin upon ruin, rout on rout'; the contrast between 'all' and 'little' in the lines, 'if all I can will serve/That little which is left'. There are many pauses, indicated by semi-colons and colons, such as after 'Confusion worse confounded;' or 'the sceptre of Old Night:', which punctuate and disrupt the smooth flow of the verse, and draw attention to phrases preceding or following. This disruption to the expectations of the verse makes the content, the words themselves, highly memorable and gives a clear indication of the highly-charged drama of the speech. Chaos uses vivid images, action verbs and long, interrupted sentences to present the dramatic nature of the vast, cosmic battle which Satan is unleashing in the universe.

6   *Have I achieved a sufficiently complex sense of the Book?*

The four passages have shown the continuing presence of one or more of the three central oppositions. What is missing, at this stage, is an examination of the central character of Satan. What I think is needed is a closer look at one of Satan's speeches, in order to see whether the oppositions of the Book are present again in everything he says. Let us look at Satan's 'acceptance speech', paragraph 13 of the summary, when he takes up the challenge of Beelzebub's proposal at the end of the debate in Pandemonium. This is a fairly lengthy piece, but remember we are only looking to extend and refine our ideas now:

> 'O Progeny of heav'n, empyreal Thrones,
> With reason hath deep silence and demur
> Seized us, though undismayed. Long is the way
> And hard, that out of hell leads up to light;
> Our prison strong, this huge convex of fire,
> Outrageous to devour, immures us round
> Ninefold, and gates of burning adamant
> Barred over us prohibit all egress.
> These passed, if any pass, the void profound
> Of unessential Night receives him next
> Wide gaping, and with utter loss of being
> Threatens him, plunged in that abortive gulf.
> If thence he scape into whatever world,
> Or unknown region, what remains him less
> Than unknown dangers and as hard escape?
> But I should ill become this throne, O Peers,
> And this imperial sovranty, adorned
> With splendour, armed with power, if aught proposed
> And judged of public moment, in the shape
> Of difficulty or danger could deter
> Me from attempting. Wherefore do I assume
> These royalties, and not refuse to reign,
> Refusing to accept as great a share
> Of hazard as of honour, due alike
> To him who reigns, and so much to him due
> Of hazard more, as he above the rest
> High honoured sits? Go therefore, mighty Powers,
> Terror of heav'n, though fall'n; intend at home,
> While here shall be our home, what best may ease
> The present misery, and render hell
> More tolerable, if there be cure or charm
> To respite or deceive, or slack the pain
> Of this ill mansion; intermit no watch
> Against a wakeful foe, while I abroad

Through all the coasts of dark destruction seek
Deliverance for us all: this enterprise
None shall partake with me.

(Book II, ll. 430–66)

a)   *Make a short statement of what the passage is about*
Satan affirms the difficult task it will be to escape from Hell, cross
the Abyss and discover what is to be found beyond. Only he can
attempt this, since he is their leader. He tells the other angels to
try to make Hell more tolerable as well as to guard it while he goes
off on his journey.

b)   *Search for an opposition or tension within the passage*
Satan draws attention to most of the negative aspects of the fallen
angels' present situation in Hell, but then becomes more positive
when he moves on to describe how he will attempt to overcome
the difficulties to be faced in escaping. His proposal reflects the
need to establish some kind of order so that they may overcome
the chaos of their downfall. He also asserts his own order over the
other angels by referring to himself in terms of the attributes of a
king who reigns 'above the rest'. Satan thus confirms his evil nature
further by usurping the attributes of God.

c)   *Analyse the details of the passage, relating them to the opposition
     already noted*
At the root of Satan's enterprise is the quest for a means of escape
from Hell in order to find a place where the fallen angels will be
able to secure a peaceful existence. The only way to achieve that
is through the totally negative path of literally declaring war upon
their present situation. The war is against God and the forces of
Heaven, the representatives of good, who are responsible for the
fallen angels being in Hell in the first place. The vocabulary of this
passage once again uses the language of royalty and imperialism
to enforce the negative aspects of Satan's character. This figure of
ultimate evil is, in truth, an imperialist warmonger, for whom the
negative means of warfare are of most interest.

The opposition between order and chaos is seen here to be
the result of Satan's wishes. He graphically describes the central
danger of the Abyss as threatening 'utter loss of being', the literal
'no thing' of chaos when existence itself may be extinguished.

Order, to Satan, principally means the order of an imperial commander, dominating others by the assumption that he is greater
than they are. Ironically, what will ensue from these orders is in
fact greater chaos. The only sort of order provided by an imperial
sovereign as devoid of the true spirit of leadership as Satan, is one
in which evil, and therefore chaos, dominates. Although Satan
confirms Beelzebub's ignorance of what may happen when he
undertakes this enterprise, he never rejects it as a course of
action. Satan's evil ego cannot permit him even to speculate on
his own position. This total *lack* of doubt is as much a negative
force as the multiple uncertainties of Beelzebub in proposing
the present course of action. All the time, Satan's driving force
is self-interest. This speech highlights the dangers of the task he is
to undertake, magnifying Satan's 'powers' in venturing into these
regions. In contrast, the tasks he leaves his supporters are menial.
Self-aggrandizement is the keynote of this speech, a fact that is
stressed when Satan closes with the words 'this enterprise/None
shall partake with me'. Satan, then, embodies the dominant oppositions of Book II, he is the figure around which they revolve.

I shall leave out steps (d) and (e) at this point in the discussion,
because much of what has already been said covers the same
ground.

Let me summarise the position this has brought us to. Book II
is clearly dominated by the figure of Satan. This is not simply a
matter of the domination of the text by a single character, but
rather points to the way Satan acts as a central focus for the major
oppositions and ideas of the poem. Book II reinforces the central
role of Satan in the whole undertaking that is *Paradise Lost*, not by
dwelling upon his characterisation, but by tying him in to all that
takes place within it.

However, what we need to do now is to try and broaden our
thinking and achieve a larger sense of the Book and its position
in the whole poem. That may sound difficult, but really it is just
a matter of examining more passages, using the method I have
employed throughout this chapter.

II   Aspects of the text

So far I have chosen passages which have helped me to build an interpretation of the text, rather than attempting a *comprehensive* investigation of the whole Book. If you are studying Book II in isolation, you should repeat the process outlined in previous pages with other passages in order to widen your interpretation. What I want to do in the next few pages is attempt to fill in one or two gaps, particularly as regards such things as character, other oppositions, and language. In my next chapter I shall deal with the background because it is important for a fuller understanding of the whole poem, but here I will concentrate further on the text.

Satan has dominated my discussions, but we have also looked briefly at Beelzebub and Chaos. I want to turn now to other figures, particularly those which take part in the debate that forms the first part of the Book. Much of the tension here arises from the differing ways in which these leaders of the fallen angels perceive their future role. The links between Belial and Mammon on the one hand, and Moloch and Beelzebub on the other, are interesting.

Mammon reveals a materialist attitude which is very much reflected in what he does, seeking for 'hidden lustre, gems and gold . . . from whence to raise Magnificence'. This portrayal becomes ironic when we find Mammon suggesting that his pro-posal may best bring about 'peaceful counsels' and 'the settled state/Of order'. Mammon represents the arguments of those who are prepared to forego the paradise that has been lost or that may lie ahead for the temporary pleasures of the 'now'. He urges the angels to make the best of the current situation. Belial proposes that the fallen angels 'sit things out', doing nothing to make their situation worse or further antagonise their opponent, hoping that all will come right in the end. While they recognise their current difficulties, it is clearly beyond the means of the fallen angels to improve them, and thus they might as well suffer them in silence, dreaming of a time when 'This horror will grow mild, this darkness light'. The problem with both of these solutions, however, is that they are extremely negative: there can be no advantage for anyone in either doing nothing or making the best of a bad deal. Moloch's argument appeals to those who see war as the only possible route out of difficulties, and Beelzebub, as we have seen, proposes a solu-tion that offers a viable alternative, while not demanding anything except from the one who volunteers to take on the task.

What is the text doing here? The fallen angels are being used to expand the concerns of the text. All four figures fail to perceive the central flaw in the proposals, which is their sustained belief in the idea that they *have* an opponent, and that the opponent is necessarily a 'tyrant'. As individual angelic figures they fail to recognise that they are in conflict with each other principally because they are approaching the problem from the wrong angle. Why? Quite simply because initially it is Satan who directs their attention towards this misconception. The four leaders of the fallen angels are totally in the control of the true tyrant who manipulates this whole debate. He has opened the council with a speech that, while its words are 'clothed with reason's garb', nevertheless clearly corrupts the outcome of the proceedings by excluding all alternative views of the matter. The purpose of the other figures in Hell is to project the figure of Satan as the one who is totally in control of everything. It is he who truly represents evil, as God represents good, manipulating his situation, his forces, their leaders, to his own selfish and vainglorious ends. The other characters, although they do have a 'life' of their own, are tools with which Satan proceeds to his goal.

Another aspect of the poem is the way in which it deals with wider issues, one of which is the role of debate in any form of government of a society. As we have just seen, Satan predetermines the outcome of the debate in Pandemonium because he bases it upon the motion of the best way to reclaim their 'just inheritance of old', and whether that way should be by means of 'open war or covert guile'. The options, in fact, are closed, the debate is sterile before it begins. The dominant figure, from the 'throne' on which he sits, appears to ask for advice from his senior colleagues, but in so doing makes only one course of action available. By further 'planting' Beelzebub amongst the speakers in this debate, he ensures that what is in fact his *own* solution to the problem is the one that is eventually accepted. The whole business is merely a parody of a society appearing to be involved with decisions crucial to its own future existence. There is no true 'community' in Hell, but rather a system based upon autocratic dictatorship with a group of individuals who are given merely the outward trappings of what we may loosely call 'democracy'. The significance of this will become clearer when we have examined the historical background in the next chapter.

There is one further aspect to be looked at, which is to do with language and imagery. I have referred to the language on a number of occasions when discussing my selected passages, indicating how it works to enhance our understanding of the text. In looking at both Book I and Book II, for example, I have noted how Milton uses the vocabulary of military affairs and aspects of monarchy to show how wrong these things are in his philosophy. The next chapter might help you to see why this is, but whenever military descriptions appear, or Satan is referred to as reigning or sitting on a throne, you need to recognise that this is placing these things in a negative light. Milton is very careful with his words, and you will rarely find one that does not have some deeper, more significant meaning when it is carefully considered. With regard to the imagery, we have seen how frequently this is used to support the meaning of the poem. The individual, long images, such as those describing Satan in Book I or the one describing the feelings of the fallen angels when they have reached their agreement in Book II (ll. 488–95) are generally referred to as *epic similes*, because they are more than simple metaphors, and carry much more than a simple metaphorical significance. Their appearance in the text should be examined closely to discover the potential ideas they contain. The same is also true of passages of description, some of which, as I have noted, can be in the *pastoral* mode, often used ironically in the opening Books, others of which will refer to classical examples to enhance their significance. I would not be too concerned with all the allusions carried by these descriptive passages, but you should note carefully how and why they help you to understand the central oppositions of the poem.

I shall leave the discussion of Book II at this point, because there is a need for us to move forward. By now you should see how the method works. A close analysis of a number of selected passages leads you to a wider perspective on the whole Book, and indicates some ideas about the overall structure of the whole poem. You may not necessarily agree with my interpretation, but the method should enable you to find a way into this highly complex text. In the next chapter I shall attempt briefly to outline the historical background to these writings, as well as to cover the essentials of the life of Milton himself. The reason for this interruption to the examination of Books of *Paradise Lost* is that by now you should have noticed that there is a concern in the text with a society that is not merely the biblical or fictional one of Hell. *Paradise Lost* also reflects a real, actual society, even if it is one that is presented through the eyes of one person, the author. If you are coming fresh to the study of Milton, your awareness of the situation in which his writings were conceived may be rather limited. The next chapter will help you to widen your knowledge, so that we may move on into the poem in a more informed way.

3
The Historical Background and the Life of Milton

The main purpose of this chapter is to provide students of Milton who may have no knowledge of the period through which he lived (1608–74) with some basic ideas about the seventeenth century. If you want to go beyond this, then a look at the short list of further reading at the end of the book will give you clues where you have to go from here. Knowledge of the period is essential to avoid making errors of judgement that will cloud a true appreciation of a text, and this is particularly important with a text such as *Paradise Lost* which relates to, and is a product of, the most turbulent political and social conditions.

I England in the seventeenth century

Three words dominate the seventeenth century in England – revolution, regicide and restoration. Allied closely to these are the concepts of king and parliament, both very different from our current understanding. What most people know is that there was a civil war, King Charles I lost and was executed, Cromwell took his place in the 'Commonwealth', but after his death the monarchy was restored with the return of Charles II. Popular history, which frequently verges on mythology, associates Cromwell with puritans and roundheads, Charles with royalists and cavaliers. 'Puritanism' as a concept is most often derided, being associated with the closure of public theatres as an example of its oppressive nature, while its followers are seen as dour, joyless individuals dressed in sombre black who spend their lives reading the Bible. The period between the execution of Charles and the restoration of his son is usually referred to as the 'interregnum', meaning between reigns. Royalist historians of the period immediately following the seventeenth century went out of their way to ensure that the time when England was not governed by a monarch was seen as the darkest period of its history, thereby ensuring public support for constitutional monarchy as the best form of government available to the people. This was particularly necessary when the throne was occupied by monarchs with only very tenuous links to the so-called royal succession.

It is important to remember that the English 'revolution', including the execution of Charles I, did not erupt overnight. Its roots lie buried deep in the sixteenth, if not the fifteenth, centuries. 'Puritanism' as an all-embracing term is pretty meaningless, except in so far as it differentiates those 'non-puritans' who supported the established Church of England, which appeared to be moving towards reconciliation with the Roman church, and those 'puritans' who felt that the English protestant reformation, which had begun during the reign of Henry VIII, had not yet been completed. Many of the religious movements of the late sixteenth and early seventeenth centuries were, in fact, probably more or less covert political movements, driven to subterfuge as a result of very oppressive government censorship. In order to explain this more fully I would like to go back to 1603.

1   The Stuarts take the throne of England

On the death of Elizabeth in 1603, James Stuart succeeded to her throne. Having been James VI of Scotland he now also became James I of England. This fact introduced a number of problems into a political scene that was already troublesome. James was a foreigner, the son of Mary Queen of Scots who had laid claim to Elizabeth's throne and who had eventually been executed by her; he spoke with a strong Scottish accent; and, perhaps worst of all, he was married to a Catholic, although he himself was a fairly convinced Protestant. James was unaccustomed to, and severely disliked, public, crowded events, and was rarely seen by the people of London. He preferred small, private, court entertainments on which he lavished a great deal of money. Disputes between those who wished to see the English church purged even further than it had been of elements of 'papist' (Catholic) practices, and those who felt that the church needed stabilising and consolidating, had been building for some years. James had ideas of becoming a 'peacemaker' in the midst of this turmoil, but he was seen too much as an isolated, 'foreign' ruler who did not really comprehend the nature of his new kingdom. Although the English people warmed to him a little after the 'Gunpowder Plot' of 1605, his attempts to arrange a marriage between his son and heir, Charles, and the Infanta of Spain depressed his already low reputation.

James ruled until 1625, in which period London, as the hub of political, religious and economic activity in England, was rapidly expanding in population though not so quickly in housing for these people. During James's reign the Elizabethan theatre, a potent force for the expression of popular political feeling in the late sixteenth century, was moving into the dark, cloistered world of the Jacobean playwrights, whose political affiliations were expressed in dramas of blood and murder. While these changes were taking place, the monarch and his court were becoming increasingly detached, and were taking on the air of a continental court associated in the English mind with flattery and Catholicism. James failed to make much headway in settling the internal debate in the English church about whether to increase or reduce reform, and the influence of Scottish presbyterian preachers and foreign protestant thinkers started to be felt more strongly in the huge number of churches then situated in London. With an English Bible now more readily available, these preachers began to show the mass of the English people that the ideas of society it contained did not often match with those of their own. Also, the same group of preachers was beginning to dominate in the educational establishments of the capital, thus spreading their reformist ideas even further.

Parliament in this period was not the permanent establishment which we understand today, but rather an occasional gathering of mostly land-owning gentlemen who would be called together by the King principally in order to finance some scheme he had devised. These MPs were mostly protestant supporters who did not think very highly of James's attempts to mediate between Protestant England and Catholic Europe, and they consequently kept him fairly short of cash for most of his reign. Parliament itself was not a constitutional organisation and the King had no need to call it at all, if he so wished, as was to become the case under

the reign of Charles, James's successor. Perhaps the most serious
disagreement between Crown and Parliament came in 1618 at
the outbreak of the Thirty Years War. On the occasions when
Parliament met, MPs had urged James to support his son-in-law,
who was the Elector Palatine and had aspirations to the throne
of Bohemia. This Protestant figure was seen as representing one
of the last bastions of Protestantism on an increasingly Catholic
continental Europe. James, however, failed to give him effective
military aid, and it seemed to his English supporters that it could
only be a matter of time before England's national independence,
as well as the property that had been acquired by these landowning
MPs after the dissolution of the monasteries, fell before the forces
of a resurgent Catholicism.

James effectively ruled by means of a tightly-knit group of
'favourites', most prominent amongst whom was the Duke of
Buckingham. It was this figure who was sent in the last years of the
second decade, together with Prince Charles, to woo the daughter
of the King of Spain. Although this alliance was rapidly rejected
when the Prince became king himself, Buckingham continued
to be extremely influential until he was assassinated in 1628.
Unlike Queen Elizabeth, James did not organize the extremely
important element of royal patronage in order to influence cul-
tural and political trends beyond the Court, primarily because
the administrative work and the political calculation this would
have demanded were alien concepts to him. As a result, the
unpopularity of the monarchy grew. It was disliked by Parliament,
which was at least in some ways a body representative of the
feelings of the English people, and alienated from the wider
potential of advisors who might have suggested more effective
courses of action than the reliance upon a few favourites who
were also heartily disliked.

With the accession of James's son Charles in 1625, matters
became worse. Charles himself had greater potential to become
popular, because he was a truly Protestant monarch, born and
bred in a Protestant England. His rejection of the Spanish alliance,
however, which could have been a point in his favour, led only to
his marriage with the daughter of the King of France. Although
this was effectively an anti-Spanish alliance, Henrietta Maria was
nevertheless still foreign, and, more important, still Catholic. She
was seen as exerting a powerful influence over her husband's

actions, particularly after the death of Buckingham, and, as a result of her position, conversions to Catholicism were not only permitted, they indeed became for a while quite the fashion. Added to this, one of Charles's chief ministers was, at the same time, both Archbishop of Canterbury and his principal advisor, thus representing the interdependence of the Church and the State. This figure was Archbishop William Laud, whose support for the conservative elements in the English church, and whose attempts to impose his views in an authoritarian manner, were the prime motivating factors in driving adherents of the reformist Church element, generally known as the Puritans, together with the Scottish presbyterians, further towards an alliance with the representatives of Parliament who feared the loss of their property. Thus religious and socio-economic movements were led to unite in a revolutionary fervour that was principally directed against the King himself and his circle of influence. For the eleven years between 1629 and 1640, Charles, together with Laud, who became effectively his Prime Minister, tried to rule England without a single recourse to Parliament. During this period, Laud succeeded in alienating a large part of the populace as well as great numbers of the clergy as a result of his highly partisan preferment of those who were his followers and his attempts to recover for the church the payment of tithes which had passed to non-clerical landowners at the time of the dissolution of the monasteries in 1547. Charles raised the finance necessary to his schemes during this period by means of extremely unpopular taxation, and even worse, added to his revenue by carrying Spanish troops in English ships to fight against the Protestant Dutch.

The end to this period of government without Parliament came when Archbishop Laud attempted to force the Church of Scotland to accept bishops, as was the established tradition of the English Church. This move, together with the imposition of a new prayer book which appeared to weaken Protestant doctrine, led to a rebellion by the Scottish aristocracy and people, so that Charles was forced to go to war against them. The army which he sent north soon proved more hostile against their own officers than the Scots, with whom they largely sympathised in this cause. In order to avoid the bankruptcy and disaster that seemed likely to ensue from this, Charles was forced to call a Parliament in November 1640.

2   Parliament is assembled, the Revolution begins

Charles in fact called a Parliament first in April 1640, but this refused to support his cause against the Scots and was dissolved after three weeks. It is known for this reason as the 'Short Parliament', as well as to distinguish it from the 'Long Parliament' which Charles was forced to call in November and which effectively was in sitting for the next twenty years. By this time Charles was held in contempt by virtually all except a small band of loyal followers, and the re-constituted Parliament was seen as representing a force that would defend religion, property and freedom. The socio-economic religious alliance had now become tied with the cause of liberty, and was thus a force that not even the king could resist.

The first major action of this parliament was the impeachment of Archbishop Laud, together with the king's principal secular minister, the Earl of Strafford. The latter was executed in 1641 and in the meantime an act was passed which would not allow for the dissolution of parliament without its own consent. Following on the death of Strafford there was a rebellion in Ireland, and parliament refused to support the king's nomination of a commander to lead an army to suppress it. This effectively forced a constitutional crisis in which the question of ultimate power in the state was raised. Parliament adopted a motion, called the Grand Remonstrance, which was a comprehensive indictment of royal policy, as a result of which the king attempted to enter the house with a body of armed men in order to arrest the parliamentarian leaders. This he failed to do, ensuring by this action the opposition of many other figures outside parliament itself, and he was forced to withdraw from London over which he had now lost control. With the extension of the constitutional situation beyond parliament and London, it was now almost inevitable that the only resolution would be through a civil war.

Although the seeds of this conflict lay many years back in English history, when it came to pass it was a fairly swift and unplanned move. The group who met in parliament in November 1640 had not planned a revolution, and still did not think that the outcome would lead to the execution of the king. There was no great revolutionary plan, and the areas of the country which refused to become embroiled in the events of the war showed that many people still considered this to be an affair which had little to do with their own lives. Communications, as such, were nowhere near the quality or quantity of those in twentieth-century Britain, and for very many people the affairs of state that were handled in London, whether by the king or by parliament, were part of a world of which they were largely ignorant.

The first battle of the war was fought between Royalist and Parliamentarian supporters at Edge Hill in October, 1642. Initially successful, the royalist forces gained some ground, but were soon overtaken by the parliamentary army who appeared to be fighting for a cause that was purposeful. By 1644 much of the north of England was in the hands of the parliamentary forces and in early 1645 the New Model Army (which came to be known as the 'roundheads' from the distinctive style of its headgear) was formed and placed under the command of Sir Thomas Fairfax. Primarily as a result of this, the royalist army was heavily defeated at the battle of Naseby in June 1645, and the war dwindled away into a series of 'mopping-up' operations. These culminated in the surrender of Oxford as the last Royalist stronghold in 1646 after the king had surrendered to the Scots.

While the war had been taking place, parliament had passed a number of acts constraining the powers of bishops in the English church, which ended in 1645 with the execution of Archbishop Laud and the abolition of the episcopacy (i.e. bishops) in 1646. Although it may appear from this very abbreviated account that the war was an orderly affair, the truth was rather different. The revolution did not develop neatly towards an aim that had been decided beforehand, but was the result of developments formed by various alliances and groupings which had many different social, political and religious ambitions. In the four years of fighting there was never anything greater than a rather sporadic series of incidents marked by a number of isolated and often inconsequential battles. Perhaps the greatest achievement was the formation of the New Model Army, which produced for the first time a national army under direct parliamentary control. It also brought about a major shift in the direction of the revolution, as the Army itself became the pace-setter, opening up the possibility of a much more radical series of social changes which were never envisaged by the original parliamentary leaders in the early 1640s.

The Scots handed over Charles to the English parliament in January 1647 and after a series of futile attempts at negotiation with the king, a court was set up and he was tried as a traitor. Having been found guilty, Charles was executed in January 1649, and England entered into a period of government that was to prove tempestuous and difficult. The monarchy and the House of Lords were abolished and England became known as a 'Commonwealth', what we might loosely call a republic today.

3 The period of the Commonwealth

Between 1647 and 1649 there was a growing awareness among members of the Army that it was they who had propelled the Revolution through its final phases. A faction within the Army allied itself with the radical views of a group known as the 'Levellers' and became increasingly concerned with the lack of progress towards democracy in the sense of universal suffrage. This factionalism eventually led to a split in the ranks of the parliamentarians between what we might term today the 'left' and the 'right'. The conservative forces attempted to disband the army in order to eradicate this split, but this only led to a greater division and eventually, in 1647, the army occupied London and forced the impeachment of the conservative parliamentary leaders. It was these conservative figures who were primarily responsible for the attempts to negotiate with the imprisoned king, hoping that they could establish a limited 'constitutional' monarchy and thereby deflect the radical democratic urges of the left. During this period, Oliver Cromwell first comes to the foreground. Initially, he supported the radical forces in the army, but after the king escaped from custody in 1647 the revolutionary forces briefly reunited in order to repel the Scottish army raised by the king. Cromwell used this as an excuse eventually to suppress the radical elements in the army, claiming that they had caused the dangerous division which led to the king's escape, and after the execution of the king in 1649 Cromwell became the dominating figure in the organisation of the government of England.

The ten-year period which was to follow is an extremely complicated one, in which power veered between Parliament and the Army, but at all times dominated by the figure of Cromwell, who was given the title of Lord Protector in 1653 by a group of army leaders known as the Major Generals. To many people this appeared to be the assumption of the role of king in all but name, and, when Cromwell began to become embroiled in European wars, Parliament became more and more opposed to him. Cromwell was gifted in maintaining a balance of power between these two forces, but it became increasingly obvious that this was a personal gift that he could not convey to a successor. He eventually nominated his son Richard to succeed him, but after his death in 1658 the conflict between the Army and Parliament came to a head. Richard abdicated in 1659 and through expediency, rather than through any real commitment to the re-introduction of the monarchy, parliament restored Charles II to the throne. The Commonwealth effectively ended in May 1660, when Charles entered England, promising that the Army would be disbanded, the rebels pardoned and a measure of religious toleration would be granted. All of these promises were eventually broken.

4   The Restoration to 1675

The final period of this short history is marked principally by the efforts made by parliament and monarch to re-establish the rule of the king in England and to begin the process which was to lead to the Commonwealth period being regarded as the 'interregnum'. Most significantly, perhaps, Charles II regarded his reign as having begun on 30th January 1649, immediately following the death of his father. A series of acts were passed in the next few years which, collectively, are known as the 'Restoration Settlements', as they attempted to deal with the outstanding matters of state. Nearly one million pounds was voted, by the parliament which continued to sit under the name of the 'Convention Parliament', in order to pay off the army. An Act of Indemnity was passed which pardoned all offences arising from the events of the preceding years, except those of fifty-seven men who were accused of regicide. Thirty of these were condemned to death, although ultimately only eleven were executed. An Act of Settlement and an Act of Explanation, passed in 1661 and 1665 respectively, attempted to settle the problems of land ownership in Ireland, although these effectively left much of the Irish land in the hands of adventurers and soldiers who became the notorious absentee Protestant landlords of Irish history. A further act arranged that all court proceedings that had started before the king's return should be continued, and confirmed all legal decisions of the Commonwealth period, thus ensuring that the constitution appeared to have 'carried through' these years uninterrupted.

In 1661 a further parliament, known as the Cavalier or Pensioner Parliament, first met, and was to continue for the next eighteen years. This was initially responsible for the passing of a group of acts together known as the 'Clarendon Code' after the Lord Chancellor of the time. The principal thrust of these acts was to ensure the exclusion of non-conformist protestants from any share in central or local government.

This period was also witness to two failed wars against the Dutch in 1665–7 and 1673–4. The first of these was blamed for a series of disasters which coincided with the two major social catastrophes of these years – the Great Plague of 1665 and the Fire of London in 1666. The first, and by far the more serious, of these, since it affected large parts of the country, is now known to have been one of many outbreaks of bubonic plague in the seventeenth century. The threat of epidemic disease was a constant factor of life at this time. Typhus, influenza and various feverish illnesses which are still often difficult to diagnose produced regular heavy death-rates, at a local or national level, throughout the period. Bubonic plague, however, was dreaded more than all other diseases. The fear in the population that was provoked by this disease was due to a number of reasons, amongst which were the suddenness of its appearance, the numbers it killed, the horror of its characteristics and the mystery, at the time, of its origins and manner of transmission. By September 1665 the epidemic was at its height, and the official recorded death toll in the City of London alone was 7165 in one week, a number which all observers agreed to be a ridiculous underestimate. Approximations of the numbers of deaths in this particular outbreak are put at more than 15% of the population of London, which gives some indication of the severity of the social disaster that was the plague.

A year after the date of the height of the plague, on 2nd September 1666, an oven in a bakery in Pudding Lane, right in the heart of an overcrowded, drought-ridden, gale-blown city of London caught fire and ignited first the building and then neighbouring houses. For three days the ensuing fire swept westward, overwhelming most of the city and parts of its suburbs. St. Paul's cathedral, eighty-seven parish churches, 13,200 houses, three markets, the financial centre of England and half of the country's greatest port were destroyed. Though there were, surprisingly, not that many deaths as a result of the fire, much of the London that had stood for seven centuries had disappeared, and it seemed to some that this was the beginning of an apocalyptic era in English history. What is more certain is that the fire caused incalculable financial damage to an economy that was already deeply problem-ridden, estimates made at or near the time suggesting damage in the region of seven to ten million pounds. National resources would now have to be consumed in the task of rebuilding the devastated city.

Little more remains to be said of this last period of our short history. Further amplification of the information I have outlined may be found elsewhere in literary and historical background material. The period following the Restoration, while in many ways it sealed the fate of the 'failed revolution' of the 1640s and 1650s, was also to see the beginnings of what is now called 'modern' British history. There were to be a number of further significant changes, most notably perhaps the so-called 'Glorious Revolution' of 1688. By the end of the seventeenth century, and despite the political upheavals and physical catastrophes, Britain was on the way to becoming the dominant world power of the following two centuries, powerful in economic and political terms, as well as playing an active role in the shaping of world events of the future.

The historical knowledge you may have gained in the last pages needs to be remembered in the context for which it was intended, and perhaps a quotation from Dr Christopher Hill, one of the most significant writers on this period in recent years, might clarify this position:

> It does not seem to me possible to understand the history of seventeenth century England without understanding its literature, any more than it is possible fully to appreciate the literature without understanding the history. (C. Hill, *Milton and the English Revolution*, p. 6)

II   The Life of John Milton

I do not intend to do more than sketch in the life of the poet in this section since my main aim is to aid you in studying the texts of Milton, rather than direct you towards biographical source-hunting. Read the following section in the light of Section I of this chapter, and this will help you place Milton in his historical situation.

John Milton was born on 9th December 1608 in Bread Street, Cheapside in London. He was the son of another John Milton who was by profession a 'scrivener', which involved the drafting of legal documents as well as dealing with a variety of financial and property transactions. The elder Milton was a relatively wealthy man, of whom the son was later to write that he was 'distinguished by the undeviating integrity of his life'. His mother, he claimed, was distinguished 'by the esteem in which she was held, and the alms which she bestowed'. Milton was educated by a succession of home tutors, amongst whom was numbered the Scottish Presbyterian, Thomas Young, from whom the young student received his knowledge of languages. In about 1620, Milton entered St. Paul's school, near to his home. This was one of a number of 'grammar schools' that had been founded in London in the previous century. From here Milton went on to study at Christ's College in Cambridge, where he appears to have been rather unhappy, claiming that the teaching at the university was not particularly to his taste. While at Cambridge, Milton wrote a considerable amount of poetry in English, Italian, Latin and Greek. He left the university in 1632 having completed his MA degree.

For the next six years Milton lived with his father, first in Hammersmith where his father had retired and later at Horton in Buckinghamshire. During this period he devoted himself to an independent programme of studies to make up for what he believed he had missed in Cambridge. He did not enter into training for any profession, nor did he become a minister of the church, which might have been expected of someone with his background and education. He did continue to write, however, and amongst the pieces he produced were the poems 'On the Morning of Christ's Nativity', 'Lycidas', and the court masque 'Comus', which was performed at Ludlow Castle on the 29th September, 1634.

In May 1638 Milton left England for a tour of Europe which was to last some fourteen months. Although this was not an unusual event for someone in his position, since it was considered a fitting completion to an education, Milton's journey was to prove remarkable principally for the people he was to prove fortunate enough to meet. His journey included visits to Paris, where he met the lawyer Hugo Grotius, author of a tragedy entitled *Adamus Exul*, from which Milton later drew material for his *Paradise Lost*; to Naples where he met Manso, who was the friend and biographer of the Italian epic poet Tasso; and to Florence, where he met Galileo, the distinguished astronomer whose discoveries included proof of the fact that the Earth was not the centre of the universe. In August 1639, Milton received news while he was in Naples that his closest friend, Charles Diodati, had died, and that a Civil War in England seemed imminent. As a result, he cut short his tour and returned to England, settling in London by 1640.

Milton now moved into a large house which he used as a private school, the pupils of which were mostly the children of his friends and relatives. It was also at this time that he became involved with the major political and religious issues of the day, and during the early 1640s his writing was mainly in prose as he published a number of controversial pamphlets, a significant and varied body of work which became the achievement for which he was best known in his own lifetime. The first five of these pamphlets were related to the dispute over Church government and the role of the bishops, in which Milton took the position of the Presbyterians in rejecting episcopacy.

The outbreak of the Civil War in 1642 coincided with a strange period in Milton's personal life. In May of that year he went to Oxford to reclaim a debt due to his father from a man called Richard Powell, but he returned home with Powell's seventeen year old daughter Mary as his wife. By July the marriage appeared to have ended as abruptly as it began and Mary Powell returned to her father's house in a strong royalist region where she was to remain for the next three years. Out of this peculiar situation came a number of Milton's most powerful and controversial pamphlets, four of which were concerned with the highly contentious issue of divorce. The other two, *Of Education*, and *Areopagitica*, were equally forthright, the latter calling for an end to all forms of censorship. As a result of these writings, Milton attracted for himself a very unenviable position as the proponent of 'divorce at pleasure', although this was not the purpose of his writings. In the event, he was reconciled with his wife in July or August of 1645, and she bore him four children, three daughters and a son who died in infancy, before she herself died in 1652.

In 1645 a book entitled *Miscellaneous Poems* collected together all that Milton had written up until that date, and although a preface to this collection compared Milton with the great Elizabethan poet Edmund Spenser it was not an immediate popular success, taking some fifteen years to sell the first edition. During the last half of the decade Milton wrote rather less, composing only a handful of poems and a number of translations of the psalms. His father died in 1647, as did his wife's father, within three months of each other. Following the execution of Charles I, Milton published a pamphlet called *The Tenure of Kings and Magistrates* which argued that a King was as accountable as any other individual to the law of the land. Shortly afterwards he was invited to become Secretary of State for Foreign Tongues, a position he held for the next six years, until ill health forced him to give up. In this post his responsibility was to write on behalf of the Council which was governing the country, supporting its policies both at home and abroad.

During this period, Milton produced a number of prose pamphlets, the principal intention of which was to support the republic against attacks mounted by European scholars engaged by the son of Charles I. Foremost among these were the two 'Defences of the English People' published in 1651 and 1654, as well as the *Eikonoklastes* (The Image Breaker) published in 1649 as a response to a text called *Eikon Basilike* which was supposed to have been written by Charles I as a defence of his own position. These pamphlets established Milton's reputation as a fierce defender of the republican system of government, and a vehement opponent of monarchy in all its forms. The so-called 'Second Defence' also included a lengthy justification of Cromwell's position as Protector, as well as a more general defence of the man himself.

During the 1650s, Milton's personal life was in turmoil. His sight deteriorated rapidly, and by 1652 he was totally blind. In the same year his wife and son died, leaving him with three young daughters, one of whom was disabled, the youngest only a few months old. He remarried in November 1656, his second wife being Katherine Woodcock, who bore a further daughter in 1657, although both

this wife and her daughter were to die early in 1658. In the
same year, Cromwell died, his son Richard took over his position,
but abdicated in May 1659. Milton published a further series
of pamphlets concerning religious freedom and against church
establishment, culminating in two versions of a text entitled *The
Ready and Easy Way to Establish a Free Commonwealth* which attacked
the institution of monarchy, on moral and on religious grounds,
on the very eve of the restoration of Charles II to the throne of
England. Milton was dismissed from office and had to go into
hiding. After the restoration, largely through the offices of his
friend and colleague, the poet Andrew Marvell, Milton escaped
very lightly from the recriminations bestowed upon the republican
sympathisers.

The remaining fourteen years of his life were devoted to the
composition of what are now seen to be his greatest works,
although he also found time to marry again, his third wife
being Elizabeth Minshall. The major epic poem *Paradise Lost* was
probably written over a four or five year period between 1658 and
1663 although it did not appear in print in its first version until
1667. In its first edition, the poem contained only ten books, which
were later expanded to form the twelve of the poem as it is now
known, published as a second edition in 1674. In 1671 Milton
published the so-called 'brief epic' *Paradise Regained*, together with
the poem *Samson Agonistes*, modelled on Greek tragedy. The first
of these was undoubtedly written during the closing years of the
1660s, but there is considerable speculation over the date of
composition of the second. On the whole, the evidence favours
a date later than *Paradise Regained*, and this is the date I shall accept
in my chapter on this poem. A new collection of Milton's shorter
poems, published in 1673, completes the appearance of most of
the works for which the poet is remembered today, although he
did continue to publish works of prose, his last pamphlet being
a defence of toleration for Protestants entitled *Of True Religion*,
published in 1673.

Milton died of gout early in November 1674 in his sixty-sixth
year. He was buried in the church of St. Giles, Cripplegate, where
his father had been buried and where Cromwell had married.
Although at first he was ridiculed by royalist sympathisers for
having taken part in the Commonwealth, Milton's reputation as
a poet grew during the following centuries, and by 1837, when a

monument was placed in 'poet's corner' in Westminster Abbey, his position was secure.

These are the basic elements of the poet's life. Once again I would stress that they present only a context into which we need place the writings. There is little real point in trawling through the life looking for evidence to support ways of interpreting the writings, and, indeed, vice versa. Many of Milton's texts, when taken out of context, would appear to show a highly contradictory and ambivalent personality, arguing, for example, for the need for an end to censorship in *Areopagitica*, although the poet became, for a brief period, the republican government's chief censor. There are many questions about elements of the life which we may never resolve, and, in some ways, that hardly matters. In the context of this book, the raw material is the texts of the poems. The life adds the necessary constraint that these are texts created by an individual at a particular point in history, and it is that context that I am now going to work into my discussion of *Paradise Lost*, Book IV. When necessary, I shall refer to the historical context outlined in this chapter to support statements about the underlying political, social or religious thrust of this poem as well as the other works. Beyond that, however, the texts remain separate from their author and the historical context, and it is for us to interpret them.

4

Paradise Lost, Book IV

I Constructing an overall analysis

We return to *Paradise Lost* by looking at Book IV, but now we may begin to extend our examination in the light of what we have learned from Chapter 3. In looking at Book IV I will continue exploring the central opposition of good and evil, but I will also show you how to draw out more interesting ideas, in particular the ways in which Satan is associated with the problem of 'power'. This, however, will come later. I should say here that I have deliberately omitted Book III as I wish to move on to those sections of the text which more commonly appear in examination syllabuses. Briefly, Book III deals with two aspects. First, God, having seen Satan journeying towards Earth, predicts the success of his endeavour and condemns mankind to death for the transgression he will make, but Christ offers himself as a ransom which God accepts. The second aspect continues Satan's journey, bringing him at last to Earth on the summit of a mountain near Eden. Book IV is a continuation of the matter outlined in Book II since it remains concerned with the development of the figure of Satan and his effect upon mankind. Book IV is fifty lines shorter than Book II, but it contains ten more verse paragraphs, making forty-one in all. The Book is divided into two sections of about two-thirds and one-third: the first section describes Satan's arrival in Paradise and introduces us to Adam and Eve, the second section is a 'discourse' or argument between Satan and the archangel Gabriel.

1 *After reading the text, think about the story and what kind of pattern you can see in it*

I'll begin with a verse paragraph summary, constructed after a first reading of the Book. This is the last time that I shall do this for you, as you should by now be confident of tackling this yourself. As a check on your developing skills, why not formulate your own summary *before* you read mine, then come back to see how close the two are.

1.   Introduction, Satan approaches Earth.
2.   Satan's first speech. He recognises the depth of evil in his rebellion against God, but purposes to continue with his intentions rather than submit himself to God's forgiveness.
3.   Satan disguises himself as he approaches Eden, but he is seen by the archangel Uriel. Paradise itself is described.
4.   Satan, finding it impossible to climb the hill on which Paradise is situated, jumps clear over the boundary, and sits in the top of the Tree of Life.
5.   The garden in Paradise is described in some detail, with its plants, trees and river which rises in the garden like a fountain. The garden is compared to those in classical writings.
6.   A detailed description of Adam and Eve together with the basis of their relationship. An account of how they spend their day.
7   Satan's second speech. He almost regrets his need to destroy these two, but places the blame for his actions on God, who has driven him to it.
8.   Satan descends from the tree and by constantly changing his shape comes closer to Adam and Eve.
9.   Adam's first speech. He praises all that God has given them, and mentions the fact that the fruit of the Tree of Knowledge is prohibited to them.
10.   Eve's first speech. She recalls the day she was created, how she saw herself in a lake and was enamoured, until a 'voice' told her of Adam, and of her meeting with him.
11.   Narrative link describing Adam and Eve embracing which inflames the watching Satan.
12.   Satan's third speech. He develops his plans as a result of what he has heard from Adam and Eve.
13.   Satan goes off to search the garden, as evening falls. The entrance to Paradise is described, guarded by Gabriel and other angels. Uriel arrives to speak to him.

14.   Uriel's first speech. He describes his discovery of Satan in Paradise.

15.   Gabriel's first speech. He suggests that he has seen no fallen angel, but he will hear of his presence, if this is true, by the following day.

16.   Uriel returns to his position near the sun.

17.   Return to the garden in Paradise as evening falls and the moon rises with the coming of night.

18.   Adam's second speech. He reminds Eve that with the arrival of the night it is time for them to sleep. Man, as opposed to the animals, needs sleep as a rest from divinely-appointed work. That work, tending and ordering the garden, is described.

19.   Eve's second speech. She acknowledges her role in life as Adam's subject. She describes the delight she finds in the world and its changing weather and times, but admits that they would be nothing without Adam. She asks why the stars shine at night when all are asleep and cannot see them.

20.   Adam's third speech. He explains the principles of day and night occurring in various, as yet unpeopled, regions of the earth. The stars shine principally to ensure that total darkness never occurs, but also to maintain a little heat in the sun's absence. They are also seen by millions of invisible creatures which exist on earth, only occasionally heard as they sing in praise of God.

21.   Adam and Eve retire to their 'bower' which is described in some detail, and seen to be greater than any equivalent in classical literature.

22.   They say a prayer to God praising Him for His gifts of the earth, their love, the garden, and for His promise that they will produce a race 'To fill the earth'.

23.   Adam and Eve get into bed and make love. In answer to critics of sexual union the narrator presents his 'Hymn to wedded love'. This praises love and sex within marriage, condemning 'casual fruition' as not befitting man's reasoning state. The paragraph closes with the plea that Adam and Eve should seek 'to know no more'.

24.   Narrative link introducing the guardian angels of the night.

25.   Gabriel issues orders to Uzziel which are enacted.

26.   Gabriel sends Ithuriel and Zephon in search of Satan.
27.   Gabriel, with his followers, Ithuriel and Zephon, comes to the bower where they discover Satan in the form of a toad sat at Eve's ear, apparently inducing base thoughts in her mind. Ithuriel touches him with his spear and he is at once transformed into his own shape.
28.   Ithuriel asks who he is and what he is doing.
29.   Satan responds contemptuously, asking why the angel does not recognise him. Zephon suggests this is because he no longer resembles his heavenly shape, and tells him he must come to Gabriel.
30.   Satan is momentarily daunted, but then resolves that he will only argue his case with Gabriel, 'the sender not the sent'.
31.   Narrative link bringing Satan before Gabriel and his guardian angels.
32.   Gabriel sees them coming and recognises Satan; he warns his companions to stand firm.
33.   The angels present Satan and tell their tale.
34.   Gabriel asks Satan why he left Hell and what he was doing in Paradise.
35.   Once again contemptuously, Satan scorns Gabriel's questions on the grounds that had their positions been reversed, he would have done likewise. He says God should have barred the exit from Hell more securely but denies he had any malign intention in Paradise.
36.   Gabriel questions Satan's 'wisdom' in that he must realise that in escaping from Hell he is likely to incur further anger, and wonders why, if Hell is so painful, only Satan has sought to escape.
37.   Satan, after mocking Gabriel's strengths, says that it is one of the true qualities of a leader to look for somewhere to settle his troops. He suggests that service of God is a much easier task than his.
38.   Gabriel pours scorn on Satan's claims to 'faithfulness', and on his mockery of their duties. He tells him to return to Hell or be dragged back there in chains.
39.   Satan challenges Gabriel to combat.
40.   Gabriel's forces form up for battle, but Satan rears up in response. But before the battle can commence God 'weighs' the outcome in a scales, and the balance falls to Satan having

to leave without a fight.

41.   Gabriel admits that force of arms will not resolve the issue; Satan recognises the sign from Heaven, and flees, taking night with him.

As before, what we need now is a shorter summary in which we can trace the poem's central ideas. Here is my version:

> Satan, having admitted the evil in his nature, arrives in Paradise. The garden and its inhabitants, including Adam and Eve, are described. Satan approaches them in disguise, overhears them talking and considers his plan of attack. His arrival is reported to Gabriel. Adam and Eve converse before retiring for the night. The angels discover Satan and bring him before Gabriel. After an argument between these two, which almost ends in violence, Satan leaves when God intervenes.

Satan, as we can clearly see from this summary, remains dominant. He is still central to the developing structure of the poem. He remains a part of the pattern of good and evil that is at the heart of the text. As the sole representative of the forces of evil here he is in opposition to Gabriel, who represents the forces of good, but he also continues to be in conflict with himself. Indeed, the Book opens with Satan stating that self-conflict, in part regretfully, but resolved to exploit it. However, Book IV introduces a further opposition – that between Satan and humanity as represented by Adam and Eve. Although Satan attempts to dodge this issue by suggesting that his quarrel with Man is only the result of his quarrel with God, the introduction of Adam and Eve adds an important quality to the pattern of oppositions. The harmony of their relationship, both in word and in deed, offers a powerful counter-thread to the structure of the whole poem. At this stage in the plot of *Paradise Lost*, Adam and Eve, who are unaware of the existence of Satan and his intentions, offer a contrasting viewpoint from which the text constructs a vision of the potential of good. Adam and Eve represent the harmony that has previously been absent from the poem, a harmony that has to be suggested by the narrative in order that Satan's disruption of it may be seen for the terrible action that it is.

**2   Select a short passage for discussion and try to build upon the ideas
you have established so far**

Once again, I shall examine three or four passages from Book IV,
beginning with a narrative passage that describes the garden in
Eden itself. The following lines, taken from paragraph 5 of the
summary, appear very early in the Book, immediately after Satan's
arrival in the garden:

> Thus was this place,
> A happy rural seat of various view;
> Groves whose rich trees wept odorous gums and balm,
> Others whose fruit burnished with golden rind
> Hung amiable, Hesperian fables true,
> If true, here only, and of delicious taste.
> Betwixt them lawns, or level downs, and flocks
> Grazing the tender herb, were interposed,
> Or palmy hillock, or the flow'ry lap
> Of some irriguous valley spread her store,
> Flow'rs of all hue, and without thorn the rose.
> Another side, umbrageous grots and caves
> Of cool recess, o'er which the mantling vine
> Lays forth her purple grape, and gently creeps
> Luxuriant; meanwhile murmuring waters fall
> Down the slope hills, dispersed, or in a lake,
> That to the fringed bank with myrtle crowned
> Her crystal mirror holds, unite their streams.
> The birds their quire apply; airs, vernal airs,
> Breathing the smell of field and grove, attune
> The trembling leaves, while universal Pan,
> Knit with the Graces and the Hours in dance,
> Led on th' eternal spring . . .
> where the Fiend
> Saw undelighted all delight, all kind
> Of living creatures new to sight and strange.
>   (Book IV, ll. 246–68, 285–7)

I shall examine this passage in exactly the same way as in previous
chapters, setting out each individual step as we come to it.

a)   *Make a short statement of what the passage is about*
This is a description of the garden in Paradise. The stress is upon its attractive, harmonious qualities.

b)   *Search for an opposition or tension within the passage*
The passage presents the opposition of good and evil through the tension existing between the aspects of harmony and order in the garden and the disorder of Satan. The evil which Satan's presence brings will lead to the loss of this place. You might also feel, however, that there is a problem here arising from the fact that this is not a 'real' description, yet the text must attempt to convince the reader that it *was* real once. The text is, in a sense, attempting the impossible by describing a perfect landscape that no longer exists.

c)   *Analyse the details of the passage, relating them to the opposition already noted*
The details support the idea of an impossibly ideal place. It is a 'seat', which suggests a number of possibilities – comfort, stability, rest, calm in terms of the more obvious meaning, but also the central feature of a kingdom or perhaps of a religious denomination, as in the 'seat of power', or the 'archbishop's seat'. The text begins to establish this place as more than a simple 'garden', which is further qualified by its being described as 'happy' and 'rural'. While the first of these adjectives is simple and direct, this is almost the first occasion in the poem when a location has been so described. It contrasts sharply with the desolation and terror we have so far experienced in the description of Hell and the Abyss. 'Rural' distances the location from anything that has to do with the work of mankind. This is clearly a place upon which man has not set his mark, and that suggestion links back to the 'happy' description in suggesting that 'happiness' preceded the fall of man, being a natural component of a divinely ordered situation. The first line of the passage itself, then, confirms the presence of the major opposition of good and evil in exploring what the garden represents. Here is a place that is truly 'innocent', that is genuinely good, which has been devised by God to be the centre of his earthly kingdom, upon the throne of which sits his ultimate creation, man.
    All through the passage the details continue to reflect this broad

theme. On one side, the view contains 'groves' which are composed of 'rich trees' whose fruit have 'golden rind', an exotic image redolent of heat and semi-legendary lands. Between these groves there are 'lawns, or level downs' on which sheep graze, an image that suggests an English landscape, cool, green and fertile. The opposition of this English and Mediterranean scene emphasises the all-encompassing, but impossible nature of the description. This is a garden in which tropical and temperate climatic conditions exist side by side in apparent harmony. The 'impossible' element of the scene is reinforced by the phrase 'and without thorn the rose', a wonderful 'throw away' idea which epitomises this vision of paradise. The rose, which is perhaps the greatest symbol of beauty in all poetry, has been utilised by authors because of the fact that its thorn-bearing branches can be seen as a metaphor of the potential *danger* of beauty. Here, the removal of these thorns removes that danger and leaves only the beauty itself. Another view reveals caves which present a welcoming aspect, offering a 'cool recess' as a shelter from the sun. This aspect is immediately followed by a description of water in a number of forms, all of which are eventually 'united'. Everything is peaceful and harmonious, without the slightest suggestion of any disruptive force to shatter this 'impossible' illusion. The main passage closes with references to birds, also in harmony, and to the air itself, completing the image of a harmonious landscape.

Into this order and harmony the text thrusts Satan, the very personification of all that embodies evil and disruption. Almost with a shock, the reader is forced to realise that the text has been describing the garden from the perspective of Satan in his position at the top of the 'Tree of Life'. This vision, filled as it is with the harmony of order and balance, resolves into the major opposition of chaos that Satan represents. The shift from an apparently neutral narrative perspective, to that of Satan, unaffected by the harmony of what he sees, once again highlights the corrupted nature of this figure. But it does more than that, for it also suggests that what the text has been conveying as 'paradise' has been mediated through the disruptive perspective of Satan. That helps the reader to the realisation that this is in fact not a 'perfect' description of perfection, but an 'imperfect' description, and that therefore the original must have been greater still.

d) *Try to say how the passage relates to the Book as a whole*
The garden continues the main opposition of the text in that
it represents the harmony, the order, of God's creation which
has been disrupted, disordered, by the powers of Satan. It is
neutral and open, filled with light and a balance of sensory
perception. There is no excess, no hint of conflict in the
natural order of the garden. You might contrast this with the
very unnatural, metallic world of Hell and its buildings, and the
presence of Satan as the figure who 'sees' this place reinforces
its distance from the chaos over which he rules in Hell. This
suggests that good is associated with nature and natural order
which is precisely what Satan sets out to destroy. The garden
in Paradise is, in effect, a large image of nature, of order,
of good.

e) *Search for anything distinctive about the passage, particularly in the
area of style, which you have not already noted*
The language of the passage owes much to the 'pastoral' idiom
noted in Book I (see Chapter 1). There it was used ironically
to describe the situation of the angels in Hell. Here it is
used to build a picture of harmony and order. The vocabulary is simple and straightforward, and the syntax relies upon
many simple phrases and clauses that do not build into complex sentences, but rather give an effect of increasing order.
Each individual item is described by means of adjectives which
encourage the sense of warmth and harmony. The groves of
trees possess 'odorous gums and balm', and fruit which hangs
'amiable'; the fields are described in an alternative phrase as
'level downs'; the hillocks are 'palmy'. This stress upon order
and harmony engages the reader's sympathy before we reach
the disruption of the Satanic perspective, and while we may
ultimately recognise that this is a flawed description of paradise,
the calming and ordering effect remains indelibly printed on the
mind's eye.
    What we need to do now is search for a further passage which
will reinforce this sense of the strength of harmony and order
in opposition to the disorder of Satan. We also need to see
the pinnacle of this example of God's creation, so I shall
look for a passage which includes some description of Adam
and Eve.

3   *Select a second passage for discussion*

This passage follows immediately after the one we have just discussed. It acts almost as the pinnacle of the description of the garden since it introduces Adam and Eve:

> Two of far nobler shape erect and tall,
> God-like erect, with native honour clad
> In naked majesty seemed lords of all,
> And worthy seemed, for in their looks divine
> The image of their glorious Maker shone,
> Truth, wisdom, sanctitude severe and pure,
> Severe but in true filial freedom placed;
> Whence true authority in men; though both
> Not equal, as their sex not equal seemed;
> For contemplation he and valour formed,
> For softness she and sweet attractive grace;
> He for God only, she for God in him.
> His fair large front and eye sublime declared
> Absolute rule; and hyacinthine locks
> Round from his parted forelock manly hung
> Clust'ring, but not beneath his shoulders broad;
> She as a veil down to the slender waist
> Her unadorned golden tresses wore
> Dishevelled, but in wanton ringlets waved
> As the vine curls his tendrils, which implied
> Subjection, but required with gentle sway,
> And by her yielded, by him best received,
> Yielded with coy submission, modest pride,
> And sweet reluctant amorous delay.
> Nor those mysterious parts were then concealed;
> Then was not guilty shame; dishonest shame
> Of Nature's works, honour dishonourable,
> Sin-bred, how have ye troubled all mankind
> With shows instead, mere shows of seeming pure,
> And banished from man's life his happiest life,
> Simplicity and spotless innocence.
> So passed they naked on, nor shunned the sight
> Of God or angel, for they thought no ill;

So hand in hand they passed, the loveliest pair
That ever since in love's embraces met,
Adam the goodliest man of men since born
His sons, the fairest of her daughters Eve.

                                    (Book IV, ll. 288–324)

a)   *Make a short statement of what the passage is about*
At least on the surface, this passage appears to be a fairly straightforward description of the two figures Adam and Eve. We are told
how they are made in God's image, the nature of their relationship
and the fact that they are both naked, and that they are walking
hand in hand in apparently perfect harmony with each other and
with their surroundings. However, this simple summary conceals
much that is of interest.

b)   *Search for an opposition or tension within the passage*
The central opposition of order or harmony and disorder is focused
on two sources: the nature of Adam and Eve's relationship, together
with the emphasis of the narrative on the fact that the two figures
are naked. There seems to be a particular narrative concern with
their naked sexual organs.

c)   *Analyse the details of the passage, relating them to the opposition
     already noted*
The tension that is created by the nakedness of Adam and Eve
emerges immediately in the opening sentence of the passage, when
the text announces that they are 'with native honour clad/In naked
majesty'. The problem here is the word 'clad' which reminds us of
the fact that as a result of the Fall we have to wear clothes. Again,
when the text returns to physical description with the account of
Adam's face we note that there is an undue concentration upon the
head and hair of the two figures. In fact, Eve's upper body appears
to be completely hidden by her hair, which is described as hanging
in 'a veil down to the slender waist'. Here the word 'veil' similarly
causes us to think, because it suggests something deliberately placed
in order to conceal, and usually out of some suggestion of modesty.
Why should this be necessary? If Eve's nakedness is majestic and
honourable, what has she to be 'modest' about? Would not this
be a *false* modesty? The final sequence, referring to what the

text coyly calls 'those mysterious parts', further emphasises the embarrassment by launching into a diatribe against what we might call loosely 'pornography' which has 'troubled all mankind/With shows instead'. How do we resolve these problems?

The simple answer is that we don't. I believe that the tension is necessary in order that the text may establish the corruptibility of these two figures. From our first encounter with them, we are receiving indications that while an overt stress is laid upon their perfection as representing humanity prior to the Fall, the problems that are inherent in human beings were present from the beginning. Adam and Eve must appear stripped of all of the faults we associate with humankind in its fallen state, but it is that very 'stripping' which reveals their fundamental imperfection. The tension of sexuality present in this passage, however, also reinforces the essential humanity of Adam and Eve, while it strives to distance itself from this for reasons of apparent modesty. The naked human form is part of the natural process of human sexual reproduction, and without the tension of sexuality engendered by that process, Adam and Eve would become neutral ciphers, against whom Satan's plotting would be meaningless.

The second source of tension is allied closely to this, as the text describes the relationship between Adam and Eve. The phrase 'both/Not equal, as their sex not equal seemed' has given critics grounds for accusing Milton of a desire to encourage the idea that man is better than woman, and much of the passage would seem to support that view. However, a point to notice is the fact that the narrative establishes a further relationship, which is that between God and Man. Both Adam and Eve are said to reveal 'The image of their glorious Maker', but the relationship is qualified as being in 'true filial freedom placed'. The word 'filial', which generates the statement in the next line, 'Whence true authority in man', reflects the essential 'masculinity' of God. Adam is a 'son' of God, as befits one male figure to another; therefore, his relationship must be more direct. There is also the suggestion that this father/son relationship is further strengthened by the need for one of man's attributes – sanctitude – to be not only 'pure', but also 'severe'. Severity, the text assures us, is not an attribute of woman, who is formed only for 'softness' and 'sweet attractive grace'. As a result of this, there is a chain of existence which runs God-Man-Woman, or, in the words of the text – 'He for God only, she for God in him'.

We, in our twentieth-century positions, may not wish to accept this rationale, but we must accept the logic that lies behind its statement here. A little further on, Eve's hair is used as a metaphor of her apparent 'subjection' to Adam, but this is again carefully qualified as being a two-way process of yielding and receiving. Eve does submit to Adam, but only because she recognises his greater authority willingly, and because he accepts her submission graciously. Again this may be difficult to accept, but we need to remember what the text is trying to establish in describing this relationship. The essential meaning of the relationship between Adam and Eve is one of harmony, and that is best described by means of a two-way process in which both individuals benefit from the presence of the other. In terms of this process, the relative 'position' of each partner is irrelevant. Where it is relevant is in making concrete the relationship between God and humanity, where a similar two-way process must operate. Humanity is subject to the authority of God, but *willingly*, not in terms of some autocratic dictator. It is Satan who introduces the conflict into this process, by suggesting that God is aiming to *deceive* Adam and Eve by means of a manipulation of his authority, which Satan perceives as being part of a malign power structure. The relationships described in the present passage offer examples of authority and subjection as benign attributes which contribute to the overall well-being of all who partake in them. It is the evil intentions of Satan which subvert this meaning and introduce the concept of power as the reason behind them.

d)   *Try to say how the passage relates to the Book as a whole*
In terms of the whole Book this passage establishes the central opposition between mankind, as represented by Adam and Eve, and Satan. What we need to note is that the conflict is carefully structured to prepare us for the downfall of man, which was predicted in the opening lines of the poem, and that it is presented in such a way that the reader may be more convinced of the plausibility and strength of Satan's actions in seeking to bring about that downfall. It is a conflict between two figures who have a genuinely harmonious relationship, even if filled with the necessary tensions of human creatures, and a figure who represents evil in consummate fashion.

e)   *Search for anything distinctive about the passage, particularly in the area of style, which you have not already noted*

All I want to say about language here is to direct your attention to the phrase near the end, 'So hand in hand they passed'. I am highlighting this because it is a notion that the whole poem manipulates very cleverly whenever Adam and Eve are present. The holding of hands is an ancient symbol of harmony, as well as a well-known convention of sixteenth and seventeenth-century love poetry, but Milton draws our attention to this matter at key moments in the text, and it is worth storing this up for future reference, particularly if you are looking at more than one Book of the poem.

Let us now move on to examine one of Satan's speeches in the first 'section' of the Book, so that we may see something of the other side of the conflict central to it. From here on, I shall not be giving you the individual steps in analysing a passage because by now you should be able to see the logical method that I am following without having to be reminded of it all the time.

4   Select a third passage for discussion

Almost at the half-way point of the first 'section', Satan reacts to his vision of Paradise and its inhabitants, principally Adam and Eve, in the following soliloquy:

> 'Sight hateful, sight tormenting! thus these two
> Imparadised in one another's arms,
> The happier Eden, shall enjoy their fill
> Of bliss on bliss, while I to hell am thrust,
> Where neither joy nor love, but fierce desire,
> Among our other torments not the least,
> Still unfulfilled with pain of longing pines;
> Yet let me not forget what I have gained
> From their own mouths. All is not theirs, it seems;
> One fatal tree there stands, of Knowledge called,
> Forbidden them to taste. Knowledge forbidden?
> Suspicious, reasonless. Why should their Lord

Envy them that? Can it be sin to know,
Can it be death? And do they only stand
By ignorance, is that their happy state,
The proof of their obedience and their faith?
O fair foundation laid whereon to build
Their ruin! Hence I will excite their minds
With more desire to know, and to reject
Envious commands, invented with design
To keep them low whom knowledge might exalt
Equal with gods. Aspiring to be such,
They taste and die; what likelier can ensue?
But first with narrow search I must walk round
This garden, and no corner leave unspied;
A chance but chance may lead where I may meet
Some wand'ring Spirit of heav'n, by fountain side,
Or in thick shade retired, from him to draw
What further would be learnt. Live while ye may,
Yet happy pair; enjoy, till I return,
Short pleasures, for long woes are to succeed.'
                                        (Book IV, ll. 505–35)

Satan is appalled by the apparent harmony of Adam and Eve, which
he sees in their obvious happiness together, but realises that he can
use God's command not to eat the fruit of the Tree of Knowledge
to destroy them.

The obvious opposition in this speech is that between the joy of
Adam and Eve and the evil of Satan's plot; but here too there is a
conflict between knowledge and ignorance. We see that knowledge
is associated with disobedience and corruption and, moreover, that
Satan identifies knowledge as a source of power, and ignorance as
its absence. As a result of this, Satan sees God in his own image – as
a tyrant.

The apparent simplicity of the opposition in this passage contrasts
with the previous passage and its quite complex tensions. The
straightforward opposition here brings us back to a level that is
easier to handle. This is all part of the enjoyment of reading Milton,
and you should not be afraid, when selecting passages, to choose
material that is 'easy' to set against rather more difficult sections.
Satan, as we have seen throughout our exploration of *Paradise Lost*
so far, is central to the text, and the narrative quite often uses this

character to display material that clarifies and simplifies the major issues. Here, by placing his power-complex at the forefront, Satan is used to highlight the reader's understanding of the opposition between knowledge and ignorance by showing that this can be a disruptive force when it is deliberately misinterpreted.

The passage suggests that knowledge, as the source of power in Satan's imagining, can be a dangerous thing. Satan suggests that Adam's and Eve's ignorance is required by God as 'proof of their obedience and their faith'. If they obey the prohibition, then they will be the servants of God, rather than His equals. Satan assumes, then, that, given the opportunity, mankind would aspire to that equality, but he is equally aware that this aspiration will cause their death. Can we question this assumption that knowledge and obedience are antagonistic? Here we must remember that Satan's aspiration to equality with God was the cause of his own downfall, and that, in one sense, his quest for knowledge resulted from his defeat in Heaven, rather than preceded it. Knowledge of his position in the structure of Heaven should have satisfied Satan, but it did not: his desire to be greater than he was led him to rebel. I think what the text is suggesting in this passage is that it is wrong to equate knowledge with power, as Satan does. His vocabulary, when considering God's prohibition, puts forward the idea that God has forbidden mankind knowledge through envy of what mankind may become if he were to become knowledgeable. Satan suggests, in a telling phrase, that the prohibition was 'invented with design/To keep them low', but this wilful misinterpretation of God's intention is wrong precisely because it associates God with Satan's conviction that He is a tyrant, whose only desire is to use His power to keep all others in subjection to Him. Because of this twisting of the 'facts', Satan reveals further aspects of his own corruption, contributing yet more to our vision of him as a figure corrupted by his own search or need for power. God's power is not tyrannical, but *just*. He does not keep man in ignorance, nor deny him knowledge, but asks him to accept his position in the order of creation which is at a point higher than other creatures but lower than the angels and God Himself. Power, it is suggested, is the disruption of order by figures who are incapable, not of accepting their lot in a fatalist way, but of recognising their role in the whole of God's plan, in which every created thing has its rightful place.

This conflict reflects questions about the nature of power which were common in Milton's society. Milton believed that all that exists is part of God's plan for creation, and human governments should seek to understand the role of humanity in God's vision. Monarchy, in the context of the seventeenth century, is allied to Satan's inability to dissociate knowledge from power. If God has planned the universe, then it could not be justified that one man should be greater than any other in terms of keeping power through the ignorance of others. Satan implies that God's actions are the result of envy and are 'Suspicious, reasonless', but this cannot be true. A human system of government that relies upon suspicion and an assumption of envy must be equally corrupt, and Milton clearly believed that the Stuart monarchs had created just such a system.

In terms of the style, Satan's speech is interesting in the dramatic qualities it possesses. The text, immediately prior to the present passage, describes Satan almost in terms of a stage direction, and the speech itself is a soliloquy, addressed to the 'audience'. It moves through a sequence of tensions as Satan recoils from the sight before him, launches into a series of rapid questions about the prohibition, rejoices at the realisation that this could be the route to his success, outlines a plan to bring this to fruition, and finally leaves to discover more, addressing a closing sentence to the two humans who are unaware of his presence. The speech is lively and attractive in delivery if not in content, and the reader may easily picture this, ironically very 'human', villain delivering his bitter aside from a position at the edge of the 'stage' that represents Paradise. Beyond the dramatic placing, of course, this also situates Satan very carefully in his place in the whole of the poem. He is forever the embittered commentator who believes that he is manipulating the action, while the text confidently reveals his true role as a disruptive force on the margins of a drama conceived by a far wiser figure than he can ever hope to be.

5   Select a fourth passage for discussion

I shall move on now to examine a further passage in which Satan speaks, but this time as part of a dialogue, the greater part of which is given to the archangel Gabriel:

To whom the warrior angel soon replied:
'To say and straight unsay, pretending first
Wise to fly pain, professing next the spy,
Argues no leader but a liar traced,
Satan, and couldst thou 'faithful' add? O name,
O sacred name of faithfulness profaned!
Faithful to whom? To thy rebellious crew?
Army of fiends, fit body to fit head;
Was this your discipline and faith engaged,
Your military obedience, to dissolve
Allegiance to th' acknowledged Power Supreme?
And thou sly hypocrite, who now wouldst seem
Patron of liberty, who more than thou
Once fawned, and cringed, and servilely adored
Heav'n's awful Monarch? Wherefore but in hope
To dispossess him, and thyself to reign?
But mark what I areed thee now: Avaunt!
Fly thither whence thou fledd'st. If from this hour
Within these hallowed limits thou appear,
Back to th' infernal pit I drag thee chained,
And seal thee so, as henceforth not to scorn
The facile gates of Hell too slightly barred.'
So threatened he, but Satan to no threats
Gave heed, but waxing more in rage replied:
'Then when I am thy captive talk of chains,
Proud limitary Cherub, but ere then
Far heavier load thyself expect to feel
From my prevailing arm, though Heaven's King
Ride on thy wings, and thou with thy compeers,
Used to the yoke, draw'st his triumphant wheels
In progress through the road of heav'n star-paved.'

                                        (Book IV, ll. 946–76)

Gabriel, speaking first (he is 'the warrior angel'), analyses Satan's previous speech in this dialogue, in which he tried to claim that he had left Hell on his own because this was the duty of

'A faithful leader, not to hazard all
Through ways of danger by himself untried.'

Gabriel scorns this argument as one reflecting selfishness rather than selflessness. He further suggests that Satan's claim to being faithful is a mockery of the term, and that his previous behaviour while he was still in Heaven was evidence of this. He tells him to leave, warning him of dreadful consequences if he refuses. Satan responds by threatening Gabriel, despite his position, suggesting that the archangel is completely in God's power.

In this passage, the central opposition is between good and evil as represented by Gabriel and Satan, but it is also strengthened by the conflict that exists between what each of these figures perceives as defining power. Satan's concept of the power of leadership is demolished by Gabriel, who also reveals that he is a powerful figure, but in a very different way from Satan. The conflict is heightened by Satan's response, when he threatens the use of power, which he claims to possess, by means of physical violence. The passage also further strengthens the central placing of Satan as a figure of corruption seduced by a vision of power which isolates him, rather than as a figure possessing a sense of responsibility.

Gabriel suggests that Satan's position when he was in Heaven was, as a result of his own hypocrisy, that of a flatterer, subjecting himself to God's authority, rather than acknowledging his position in the order of creation. He suggests that no angel was worse than Satan in that he

'Once fawned, and cringed, and servilely adored
Heav'n's awful Monarch.'

Satan's actions were not only corrupt in action but in conception – not being a creative force it is impossible for him to 'displace' God. Gabriel's argument therefore adds a further level to our understanding of Satan and his position in the Book. As well as the actual evil that we have seen in his intentions to revenge himself against God, we now learn that the root of those intentions was false also. Satan *will* not succeed in his final intention – to achieve ultimate power – because he *could* not succeed in this impossible quest. It is his failure to realise this fact that destroys any lingering sympathy the reader may have for him. Satan's response to Gabriel's words reveals the depth of his ignorance of an understanding of power as he boastfully threatens Gabriel, scorning him as a beast of burden, 'Used to the yoke', doing no more than pulling God's chariot through the heavens. If any figure is in thrall, it is Satan, transfixed by his vision of attaining a position of power greater than God, reduced to a pathetic bully, blustering his way out of a difficult situation.

Turning to the dramatic quality of the interchange in this passage, I think I would again underline the ways in which the speeches would work as a piece of stagecraft. Once again the two figures are 'humanised' in the sense that they speak as actors might do. Gabriel's speech also contains the sequence of dramatic tensions that we noted in Satan's speech in the previous passage. There are the numerous half-direct, half-rhetorical questions, which address themselves as much to the reader in his or her role as 'audience', as they do to Satan. There are the alternating patterns of statement and exclamation as in the line, 'But mark what I areed thee now: Avaunt!', which carry physical movement within them like a hidden stage direction. What is added in this passage, however, is a much greater sense of the potency of dialogue, particularly noticeable in the epithets they throw at each other, such as 'thou sly hypocrite', 'Proud limitary cherub'. The dramatic tension of this dialogue further enhances the reader's awareness of the impossibility of actually arguing or discussing any matter with Satan, whose ideas are fixed, and whose main weapon of discourse is scorn and a contemptuous disregard for the opinions of his opponent. This last word is significant here – Satan cannot carry on a 'conversation', he must always have what amounts to a dispute.

6   *Have I achieved a sufficiently complex sense of the Book?*

The first extract I chose showed that narrative description plays a part in establishing a context for the presentation of ideas. Looking back, I can see that 'power' is clearly established as a central issue in Book IV by means of the *vocabulary* applied to the description of the garden. Adam and Eve, presented as the chief inhabitants of this place, enable the text to reveal the harmony of Paradise by means of references to *order*. That order is as God planned the universe, not with everything equal, but with everything fitting into a large design that all created things should recognise and accept. The divine order of creation does not mean a tyrannical regime in which everything is *subject* to the creature next above it, but rather that God has constructed a vertical universe with Himself as the highest feature. This is justifiable because He created it all, and there follows a clearly marked sequence of creatures beneath Him, each acknowledging its position within the structure.

The other passages further enhance the reader's understanding of the concern there is in Book IV with these questions of power and order. Gabriel, representing an ordered universe, does not wield power, but handles it. He addresses himself to the question of the nature of true power by comparing Satan's actions with the evidence of God's power. The text is, therefore, justifying God's ways, exploring the meaning of a just power, as compared to a corrupt and corrupting power. God is the supreme power without question, a position which He does not need to maintain by means of physical violence. There is a necessary tension in the idea of power, but it can be resolved if it is understood as the driving force behind a state of order and balance. Satan's wilful misunderstanding, or perhaps deliberate misinterpretation, of the notion of power has created for him an unbalanced state in which power has to be exerted rather than accepted. His attack upon Adam and Eve arises from this position, and he will achieve his aim by producing in the human couple a similar sense of unbalance. Their relationship is carefully structured upon a system of relative positions which they freely accept – disturb the balance of that system, and disorder will inevitably follow.

Satan's misuse of power sparked disorder in the structure that God had created, and the only solution was to remove that disorder, as happened when Satan was banished to Hell. Satan's response to Gabriel's words in the last passage only really serves to reinforce these matters. He believes that he is not actually Gabriel's 'prisoner' because he is not in 'chains', and that the archangel is therefore powerless against him. Satan can only perceive of power as being restrictive and confining, but Gabriel's power is not corrupt, it is just – he does not need to restrain Satan physically, exactly as God does not need to enforce physically allegiance to Himself in Heaven. In the same way He does not need to constrain physically Adam and Eve from eating the forbidden fruit. All are free to reject order or balance, none are *forced* to acknowledge them.

II   Aspects of the Book

My choice of extracts has tended to highlight only one or two of the central features of Book IV. There are others, and again I would stress that if you are studying the Book as a single unit you would need to repeat the process in order to clarify these. I have concentrated my attention on the central oppositions such as good and evil, knowledge and ignorance, and on the text's development of the figure of Satan.

It is Satan alone who cannot accept his role in the universal order and, after corrupting the fallen angels, he has disrupted God's plan by rebelling. Book IV stresses the fact that Satan did so as a result of the *free will* that God had given to him when he was created. Satan was never forced to acknowledge the position of God, he simply had to accept the *justice* of the created order. Adam and Eve, when the text first presents them, freely acknowledge this order and are prepared to live by it because of the benefits it brings them. The text also stresses the fact that they too have free will, which is constantly 'tested' by the presence of God's prohibition against eating the fruit of the forbidden tree. Satan's recognition of this freedom of choice leads him to outline his plan of action because he cannot accept that *authority* is willingly acknowledged.

As we saw in the discussion above in Step 6, power is presented in Book IV as a central aspect of the development of the plot. Each creature in the divine order of creation does not, as Satan believes, subject itself unwillingly to the authority of those greater than itself, nor is it in any way constrained or forced to accept that authority. Rather, divine order is a contract entered upon completely freely by all creatures, who may, at any point, should they so wish, opt out. The whole purpose of the text is to reinforce the idea that there should be no need to opt out, unless for reasons that are effectively corrupt, arising from a misunderstanding or a misinterpretation of the order of creation. Satan has chosen to do so because he has misconstrued the meaning of 'power', believing that this is a force to be utilised against other creatures, rather than seeing it as a benign attribute of justifiable authority.

You may also note, after the outline given in the previous chapter, that Satan's eternal quest for power, principally as it may be used against weaker creatures than himself, is presented as a kind of *metaphor* for the power struggles that dominated English society in the seventeenth century. There is no need to turn *Paradise Lost* into some kind of allegory, as I have said earlier, because that is not the point. The metaphor is much more effective if it is understood as questioning the whole motivation of those who seek power in order to manipulate others. Milton's vision of a just society does not include the idea of 'equality' in a twentieth-century sense because that would leave no place for God as the supreme figure which He has to be. What that vision does suggest is that human society must be seen as a part of the much greater order that is God's universe. There may well be gradations of authority, but only when freely acknowledged by all fully participating members who have accepted their roles and are not subject to the tyranny of those above them.

The problem is that one creature opting out of this divine order can cause chaos, as the disruption will inevitably filter down through the system. In *Paradise Lost*, Satan is that individual, and the chaos ensuing from his actions is the fall of man and the disruption of human history until it is rectified by the intervention of Christ, who freely offers himself as the sacrifice needed to begin to restore the order that has been lost. Books IX and X of the poem deal specifically with the fall of man and its immediate aftermath, and it is to this point in the text that I shall turn in my next chapter.

5
Paradise Lost, Books IX and X

I Constructing an overall analysis

Books IX and X of *Paradise Lost* unfold what is the central drama of
the whole poem – the temptation and fall of Adam and Eve. They
are often studied as a single unit for the purpose of examinations,
and therefore I shall take the two Books together. This does mean,
though, that I will have to confine myself to a tighter analysis of
their features. These Books return the reader to Satan's attempt
to disrupt the harmony and order of Paradise through corrupting
Adam and Eve. Taken together, Books IX and X contain nearly
2300 lines of verse. You would be wise to begin by constructing a
verse paragraph summary, in order to grasp the essential matter
of these Books, after you have read through them at least once. I
shall not offer my own summary here, because you should see how
to do this by yourself, using my earlier summaries as a guide if you
feel the need. Having done this, try to encompass the whole sweep
of the material, getting into your mind as straightforward a picture
of the important elements as possible, so that you can move on
comfortably to the first section of this chapter. Without doing this,
you may find my choice of extracts more confusing than helpful.

In the last chapter I began to indicate some of the ways in which
the issues considered in *Paradise Lost* may be seen as reflecting
important issues in the seventeenth century. These have been
well described by Christopher Hill in his book *Milton and the
English Revolution* where he argues that *Paradise Lost*, like Milton's
other great writings of the same period (*Paradise Regained* and
Samson Agonistes), is a deeply political text. Hill states that the
poem wrestles with a number of problems, but principally the
failure of the revolution of the mid-seventeenth century, and the
non-appearance of the anticipated 'millennium' when, according
to biblical and other sources, the 'end of the world' would come

about. The problem in making a statement of this kind, however, is twofold. First is the rather 'limiting' interpretation that many students put upon the word 'political' today, often associating this with twentieth-century 'party politics' of the Left and the Right, Tory, Labour, etc. Second, there is the danger in a political reading of allegorizing the text, or developing a reading which supports a particular, pre-conceived set of political ideas by means of deliberate rejection of possible alternatives. For the student new to Milton, struggling to come to terms with the apparent complexity of *Paradise Lost*, a 'political' reading offers either further confusion or a simplistic escape route which tries to identify Satan with Charles I or Cromwell, or even Milton himself, by means of injudicious selection of material taken out of context. Nevertheless, an understanding of the 'political' aspect of the poem is necessary if it is to become more than an historical artefact, worthy but ultimately rather dull. In this chapter, I want to try to develop that aspect in one particular way, in order to indicate how this approach may further strengthen our appreciation of this astonishing piece of writing.

1   *After reading the text, think about the story and what kind of pattern you can see in it*

First, a brief summary of the contents of Books IX and X:

IX   Satan returns to Paradise and enters the serpent. Adam and Eve, after a discussion over the nature of the work they are required to do, go their separate ways in the garden; although Adam is very reluctant to allow this he is persuaded by Eve. Satan, in the guise of the serpent, approaches Eve and flatters her into eating the fruit of the forbidden tree of knowledge. Eve, initially elated at the effect, brings the fruit to Adam, who is at first appalled, but then accepts because of his love for Eve. After an initial delight, both realise their folly and accuse the other of bringing about their downfall.

X   The disobedience is discovered by the guardian angels who return to Heaven to report this to God. God's Son comes to

Earth and condemns Adam and Eve to death after expulsion
from Paradise. Sin and Death, Satan's offspring, build a
bridge across the Abyss over which they pass to the Earth.
Satan returns to Hell, boasts of his success, but the fallen
angels are transformed into serpents and are forced to
eat 'dust and bitter ashes' in a parody of Adam and Eve's
eating of the forbidden fruit. God foretells his Son's eventual
conquering of Sin and Death, while Adam and Eve lament
their fate. They are finally partially reconciled by the Son's
promise that their descendants will be revenged upon Satan
and they seek to find forgiveness from God.

In both Books the pattern of good versus evil continues. Now,
evil is overcoming good and by bringing about its downfall creating
a further pattern which establishes the consequences of this. Sin
and Death emerge as the victors in this conflict. Yet the close of
Book X notes that all has not been plunged into eternal darkness,
for God reveals that he has a plan to defeat Sin and Death, through
Christ, and Adam and Eve begin to develop a new relationship with
each other and with God. In these two Books, chaos comes nearest
to success, but the order which God represents still manages to
reassert itself. In the widest sense of the word, the changes which
take place in human ways of living, in relationships with God, and in
God's plans for the future, can be seen as 'political'. In this context,
'political' means the ways in which human beings associate with
themselves, organise themselves, and maintain or change structures
which will benefit all members of a 'society'. The political aspects of
a human society are those which relate to the government of the
society, the rules it has, the ways in which it treats rule-breakers, the
treatment of wrong-doers. Order is therefore a very political idea,
and God's reassertion of order over the chaos brought about by
Satan is a political action. Events in seventeenth-century England
had clearly shown that both religion and politics were tied up with
the whole idea of order.

Let us, then, look at a number of passages which show that this
is a perspective present in the poem. In thinking about the pattern
here we are extending our reading by looking for a particular
pattern, rather than simply allowing one to arise. This does *not*
mean, however, that we are seeking to *impose* a pattern on the text.
The summary of Books IX and X shows this political pattern. Adam

and Eve, in *Paradise Lost*, represent human society. Their discussions and actions in Book IX are a kind of microcosm of social structures. There is a debate on the nature of how their society is to be seen, as a single unit, or as two parts of a whole. Let us begin there.

2   *Select a short passage for discussion and try to build upon the ideas you have established so far*

The full 'debate' between Adam and Eve is fairly lengthy, running to some one hundred and eighty lines of text. What I can indicate here, by looking at one of the speeches, is the nature of the argument. This passage is Adam's final contribution, at the end of which he accepts Eve's proposition that they should separate and go off to work on their own for a short period:

> 'O woman, best are all things as the will
> Of God ordained them; his creating hand
> Nothing imperfect or deficient left
> Of all that he created, much less man,
> Or aught that might his happy state secure,
> Secure from outward force: within himself
> The danger lies, yet lies within his power;
> Against his will he can receive no harm.
> But God left free the will, for what obeys
> Reason is free, and reason he made right,
> But bid her well beware, and still erect,
> Lest by some fair appearing good surprised
> She dictate false, and misinform the will
> To do what God expressly hath forbid.
> Not then mistrust, but tender love enjoins,
> That I should mind thee oft, and mind thou me.
> Firm we subsist, yet possible to swerve,
> Since reason not impossibly may meet
> Some specious object by the foe suborned,
> And fall into deception unaware,
> Not keeping strictest watch, as she was warned.
> Seek not temptation then, which to avoid

Were better, and most likely if from me
Thou sever not; trial will come unsought.
Wouldst thou approve thy constancy, approve
First thy obedience; th' other who can know,
Not seeing thee attempted, who attest?
But if thou think trial unsought may find
Us both securer than thus warned thou seem'st,
Go; for thy stay, not free, absents thee more;
Go in thy native innocence, rely
On what thou hast of virtue, summon all,
For God towards thee hath done his part, do thine.'

                                        (Book IX, ll. 343–75)

Adam's argument at this point in the debate is quite complex. He
rebuts Eve's previous point that God may have made certain things
imperfectly, reiterating his central concept that they alone may
make the wrong choice because of a potential conflict between
reason and will. Reason may be duped by an enemy and cause
the will to transgress. He asserts that they should remain together
because their love will form the best defence, and asks her not to
look for temptation, which is likely to come anyway. In the end,
however, he must allow her to go if she wishes, because he cannot
force her to stay against her will.

The major opposition of this passage is that between the individual and society, and Adam's discourse develops a number of
the problems that are central to this. Should individuals within a
social grouping remain together in order to provide the best form
of defence against an unknown 'enemy', or should they trust the
strength of individuals to survive, at least temporarily, outside that
society? The reasons which Adam gives for allowing Eve to go if she
wishes are also important, because they again indicate the problem
faced by societies which may wish to constrain individual members
against their will. But if Eve is more vulnerable on her own, are we
to assume that the same is true of Adam? Or does his position in
the created hierarchy preclude that assumption? If the stronger
members of a society allow the weaker to reject their advice because
they do not wish to constrain them by force, is that an indication of
strength, or weakness? What makes the whole issue more interesting
in the present context is the reader's acute knowledge that Adam's
words are virtually a prophecy of ensuing events. As a result of what

happens in the rest of Book IX, Adam is shown to be 'right', but the text is clearly creating a tension here in that Adam himself is only *speculating* – he has no real foreknowledge. In political terms, hindsight is often a wonderful tool for developing theories which may not have even been considered prior to the events which ultimately ensue.

Adam's speech begins by establishing the centrality of God's position in all things. The vital phrase is 'as the will/Of God ordained them', which clearly shows that there is an order and a meaning to everything. This is the principal foundation for the whole of Milton's interpretation of human political thinking, as I indicated earlier. We cannot look at the world about us and claim that, if something appears to be wrong, it must be God's fault. In the context of the failure of the seventeenth-century revolution, with Charles II having been returned to the throne, this point needed to be reiterated again and again, as Milton attempted to show that it was the revolutionaries who were at fault, and not God for having permitted them to fail.

Milton's Adam is often accused of being weak and vacillating, presenting cogent and coherent arguments why Eve should remain with him, but nevertheless allowing her to go. On the contrary, I would suggest, this passage indicates the predicament of all human debate, which is that argument should seek to persuade by means of rational material, but a reasonable human being should also be aware of the tensions that are inherent in anything proposed. The only way in which Adam can actually stop Eve is physically to restrain her, and that is not an action open to him in his pre-fallen state, nor should it be even after the Fall. True debate sets reason against reason, it does not set will against will. Adam's real problem may be that Eve's will *is* set against him, and that there is nothing he can *reasonably* do to make her change her mind.

In terms of the whole Book this passage indicates that Eve's temptation and fall is virtually inevitable, but it does also show that she goes to her fate willingly and with the acceptance of Adam, though he regrets this. The whole point is that their fate will not be imposed upon them by a superior force; Satan will not be a super-human destructive figure who simply dominates an inferior force, and that is important for the reader's understanding of the underlying principles of the poem. As a part of the debate, Adam's speech is not that of a weak-willed man dominated by the

will of his wife, but an example of how humanity often enters into
the unknown, conscious of dangers that may be present, but having
at least presented arguments that recognise these dangers and warn
against them. In the wider context, this passage presents some of
the reasons why the English revolution failed, even though Milton,
and others of its supporters, believed unswervingly in the justice of
its ideas. The revolutionaries, according to this reading, failed to
present sufficiently powerful arguments against the restoration of
the monarchy, as well as failing to present the case for the republic.
But they certainly could not therefore turn to violence in order
to maintain their position, which would have forced the English
people to act against their will, no matter how deluded they may
have appeared to be.

We have seen, then, how the passage operates on a number
of levels, each tightly enmeshed with the others. The speech,
and the debate of which it forms a part, contributes to the
reader's understanding of the impending chaos by enlarging the
vision from that of a futile mistake perpetrated by two ignorant
individuals to the more coherent one of a social structure under
impossible pressures that cracks apart despite the attempts made by
the individuals to avoid destruction. In this way, the fall of Adam and
Eve becomes a metaphor of all human, social and political failure.
I shall move on further into Book IX now and look briefly at some
other passages.

3   Select a second passage for discussion

As may be seen from the summary, Eve leaves Adam's side, goes
off alone, is met by Satan in the guise of a serpent, is tempted to
eat the forbidden fruit and does so. She returns to Adam who
also eats the fruit, having decided to throw in his lot with Eve
rather than risk living alone without her. After an initial and brief
enjoyment of their actions, Book IX reveals a return to debate
in the closing lines. Now, however, the debate is accusatory and
rancorous, both Adam and Eve accusing each other of being the
cause of the transgression. The following passage, containing part
of the contribution made by each figure, appears almost at the end
of the Book:

To whom, soon moved with touch of blame, thus Eve:
'What words have passed thy lips, Adam severe!
Imput'st thou that to my default, or will
Of wand'ring, as thou call'st it, which who knows
But might as ill have happened thou being by,
Or to thyself perhaps? Hadst thou been there,
Or here th' attempt, thou couldst not have discerned
Fraud in the Serpent, speaking as he spake;
No ground of enmity between us known
Why he should mean me ill, or seek to harm.
Was I to have never parted from thy side?
As good have grown there still a lifeless rib.
Being as I am, why didst not thou, the head,
Command me absolutely not to go,
Going into such danger as thou saidst?
Too facile then, thou didst not much gainsay,
Nay didst permit, approve, and fair dismiss.
Hadst thou been firm and fixed in thy dissent,
Neither had I transgressed, nor thou with me.'
To whom then first incensed Adam replied,
'Is this the love, is this the recompense
Of mine to thee, ingrateful Eve, expressed
Immutable when thou wert lost, not I,
Who might have lived and joyed immortal bliss,
Yet willingly chose rather death with thee?
And am I now upbraided, as the cause
Of thy transgressing? Not enough severe,
It seems, in thy restraint. What could I more?
I warned thee, I admonished thee, foretold
The danger, and the lurking enemy
That lay in wait; beyond this had been force,
And force upon free will hath here no place.'
                              (Book IX, ll. 1143–74)

Eve rejects Adam's accusation that if she had listened to his advice
she would not have been tempted by suggesting that it would
have happened wherever they were, whether together or alone.
He would have been seduced by the Serpent's words as much as
she was. She then asks whether they should have always had to be
together, and finally accuses him of not having been sufficiently

authoritarian as to have insisted on her staying. Adam's response is rather petulant to begin with, suggesting that Eve shows little gratitude for the fact that he has thrown in his lot with her. He asks what more he could have done to stop her leaving, returning to his point about the impossibility of imposing his will on hers by force.

What are we to make of this, which is now much more an angry dispute, rather than a reasoned debate? The central opposition is between the two figures themselves, neither of whom present reasoned arguments any longer, but use their own ideas raised previously to attack the other's. A deeper tension arises precisely from the breakdown of the reasoned debate itself. The passage is an example of human discourse at its worst, when each speaker accuses the other of being at fault without presenting a coherent argument. In a political sense the passage represents the outcome of a breakdown in social structures, when the injured parties remonstrate with each other, regardless of the fact that the true cause of the disruption – in this case Satan – has been left to rejoice over his success in causing the chaos. It is an example of the disorder that inevitably follows disruption, when man's vision becomes distorted, blinkered and irrational.

Eve's speech indicates the breakdown in the first line, when she addresses him as 'Adam severe' because of his previous words. Prior to the fall she had spoken to him with phrases such as 'Offspring of heav'n and earth, and all earth's lord', but now the tone is accusing and admonishing. The word 'severe' is also deeply ironic in that, by the end of her speech, Eve is suggesting Adam was at fault because he was not severe enough with her before she left his side. Worse than that, she believes that Adam would have probably also been fooled by Satan's words, which is the counter to Adam's suggestion that he has access to 'right reason'. She excuses the serpent's duplicity by suggesting that she had no reason to believe that the creature should wish her ill, an interesting idea in itself. The structure of their society is now collapsing because, Eve is suggesting, there was neither strength in combination, nor in the acknowledged superiority of the male figure.

She also questions the whole problem of what exactly a 'society' means. Eve suggests that without independence she is nothing, 'still a lifeless rib', although that independence appears to have contributed to her downfall. In terms of the political structure, here the tension is between social units and the independence of the individual within these. Is a society composed of individuals whose movements are not governed by the needs of the unit, or are those individuals totally subjugated when they are seen as part of the structure? Although only touched upon, this is a fascinating political problem for any commentator attempting to resolve the opposition between the individual and society. From here Eve moves to her final point which relates to the question of command and authority. The language used in the closing lines echoes precisely the problems inherent in the tensions of political structures. She asks why Adam did not 'Command me absolutely', she suggests he was 'Too facile', that he 'didst permit, approve and fair dismiss' her, and that he was not 'firm and fixed in [his] dissent'. It is easy to see how these ideas may be applied to any political structure at any point in history, and it is, again, the central tension that underpins any system of government. How far must a governing body permit the individual liberty to commit acts of wrongdoing, before it restrains those individuals from acting in ways likely to be detrimental to their own well-being? You might like to think of the problems caused by the Prohibition of Alcohol Acts of the United States in this century, or those encountered by our own government as regards the consumption of tobacco.

Adam's response to Eve's accusations is not immediately to reason with her, as should be the case in an ordered debate, but to be petulant and selfish. His 'I would have been better off without you' attitude again signals the breakdown in this society, as he resorts to futile gestures which do not affirm or advance his position. He also, and this is more damaging, fails to recognise that the primary cause of their transgression was not themselves, but Satan, and turns instead to excusing himself from not having been 'enough severe'. His argument, in itself, is correct here, because he rightly acknowledges the fact that 'force upon free will hath here no place', a point that was implicit in the earlier speech we looked at. The political tension rests in that prohibition. No governing body should have to resort to force in order to impose its will, because the mere act of doing so restricts the free will of others. The root of the problem relates to the governance of any social structure. If a government cannot resort to force, and its reasoned arguments are rejected, must disruption inevitably follow? In Adam's argument the answer would appear to be 'yes'. However, the text emphasises that refusal to confront the transgression squarely, and to seek for it, is the true cause.

In the wider context of Book IX, we can perhaps begin to see the effect of the Fall, in exactly the same way as we saw the build-up to it. Adam's and Eve's eating of the forbidden fruit is important in the literal sense that this is a deliberate act of disobedience against God in order to gain knowledge and therefore, presumably, power. It is also metaphorical of human society making the wrong political decisions, despite an awareness of the potentially disastrous consequences, and thus being thrown into a state of chaos, in which no decisions may be made, because those who suffer the consequences do not seek to correct their failings, but rather prefer to wag accusing fingers at each other. The English revolutionaries were guilty of just such actions in the 1650s, and, perhaps more particularly, in the short period after Cromwell's death, when his son was leading the 'Protectorate'. They, as it were, ignored the root cause, which was corrupt monarchical government, and instead turned to bickering among themselves, disintegrating into factions that proposed increasingly fewer reasonable solutions.

The summary of Book X indicated that a possible solution to this problem of human political failure is offered in the judgement of the Son. I shall now look for a passage which relates to that in order to develop my points.

4   Select a third passage for discussion

Rather than examine a single piece here, I have selected two shorter passages from the opening lines of Book X. This is because the ideas that are put into the mouth of the figure of the Son of God tend to be distributed over a wider range than is usual. The Son accepts God's request that He go to judge Adam and Eve after the Fall with the following words:

'Father Eternal, thine is to decree,
Mine both in heav'n and earth to do thy will
Supreme, that thou in me thy Son beloved
May'st ever rest well pleased. I go to judge
On earth these thy transgressors; but thou know'st,
Whoever judged, the worst on me must light,
When time shall be; for so I undertook
Before thee, and not repenting, this obtain
Of right, that I may mitigate their doom
On me derived; yet I shall temper so
Justice with mercy as may illustrate most
Them fully satisfied, and thee appease.
Attendance none shall need, nor train, where none
Are to behold the judgement but the judged,
Those two; the third best absent is condemned,
Convict by flight, and rebel to all law;
Conviction to the Serpent none belongs.'
                              (Book X, ll. 68–84)

When He arrives in Paradise He questions Adam and Eve over what
they have done, and when Adam tries to put the whole blame for
their actions on the head of Eve, the Son replies,

'Was she thy God, that her thou didst obey
Before his voice, or was she made thy guide,
Superior, or but equal, that to her
Thou didst resign thy manhood, and the place
Wherein God set thee above her, made of thee
And for thee, whose perfection far excelled
Hers in all real dignity? Adorned
She was indeed, and lovely to attract
Thy love, not thy subjection, and her gifts
Were such as under government well seemed,
Unseemly to bear rule, which was thy part
And person, hadst thou known thyself aright.'
                              (Book X, ll. 145–56)

These speeches both offer an insight into a specifically Christian
view of social and political structures. In the first, the Son accepts
completely His Father's decree, but stresses that whatever may be

the judgement, it is one that He will ultimately also suffer since He has offered Himself in payment beforehand. He will ensure that 'Justice with mercy' is carefully balanced, and He states that He alone will carry out the judgement on Adam and Eve. The second speech is a direct response to Adam's attempt to excuse himself from the blame of the Fall. The Son clearly re-states the divine order of existence in which Man and Woman have their rightful places, not as equals, but as rungs on the ladder. Finally He makes explicit the point that the root cause of Adam's failure was his lack of self-knowledge.

The central interest in these two passages lies in their clear restatement of the opposition between order and chaos, and their implicit restatement of the need to resolve the tension that arises from the opposition between the individual and his or her society. The Son's response to His Father's mission is couched in a language that is at once humble and strong. The Son accepts, without question, His role as the actual judge, but is firm in His intention to be merciful in the execution of that judgement. His humility, in being prepared to enact God's decree that Adam and Eve must die as a result of their transgression even though He knows He must suffer the same fate, contrasts vividly with Satan's rejection of his sentence in the earlier Books of the poem. Yet the affirmation of the need for mercy recognises that He also has free will, which He is prepared to implement in order to temper the divine decree. The Son's response to Adam, in a similar way, admonishes Adam for his rather feeble attempt at excusing himself, but does so by means of establishing the irrational nature of Adam's plea. He reasserts the need for an accepted order, the existence of which has been rejected, and stresses the failure of Adam himself, a factor which the latter has been unable to admit.

The political dimension here relates to the idea of justice. You could perhaps think of how society's laws are constructed in such a way as to act as a 'deterrent' to others, whereas the Christian attitude to justice should be more concerned with correcting the faults of individuals for their own sake, rather than to put off others. In the widest sense, the Son's words are an attempt to establish a judicial system within a political framework which accepts the inevitability of transgression, but does not seek to maintain that framework by means of a fear of the outcome for those who do transgress. This is often to be seen in discussions of the role of the prison system in a modern, civilized society, where there is a constant tension between those who seek to punish and those who seek to reform. The Son takes the 'reforming' position, which is always conscious of the potential for re-integration of those who are at fault in some way. It is for this reason, I would suggest, that the speech closes with the outright condemnation of the main evil figure, because he is 'rebel to all law'. Society needs laws, it needs to recognise that there may be individuals who may break those laws, but it cannot accept those who reject them all.

But there is another problem here. Adam's words suggest that he allowed Eve to become his 'superior', thereby usurping the place of God in the order of things, or that he allowed her to become 'but equal', which is also a fault. This idea may appear difficult to a twentieth-century reader since it contradicts our idea of gender equality, but the Son's point is that Adam has reversed or rejected God's plan, and that is his fault. He is careful to remind Adam, and the reader, that Eve has her qualities, she is 'Adorned', and 'lovely to attract/Thy love', but the main thrust of the argument is that these qualities 'well seemed' only when 'under government'. The implicit metaphor here relates to the political structure which Adam and Eve represent. In disrupting that, the chaos of the Fall has been allowed to happen, and this occurred principally because Adam had not 'known thyself aright'. Self-knowledge, it seems, is the key to the Christian understanding of the role of the individual in society. True knowledge of one's self, rightly acknowledged, will enable both the individual and the society to flourish, because the relationship is reciprocal. In criticising Adam's excuse, the Son puts forward a clear, explicit statement of the necessary political structure which has God as its head, and all other created beings in their respective positions afterwards. This is not the tyrannical subjection of the individual, which is what Satan would attribute to God's plan, and which, Milton believed, was the problem behind the monarchist governments prior to the revolution, but a creative, acknowledged and fully accepted order of existence, as established by the Son in His relationship with and to His Father.

The remainder of Book X effectively deals with Adam's and Eve's growing awareness of their new situation, which leads eventually to their joint return to the place of judgement in order to seek God's forgiveness. By the end of this Book, they have begun the process of regaining self-knowledge, in order that they may continue with their lives, rebuilding a semblance of order in the world that has been given them as a punishment for their transgression. In order to emphasise by contrast this need for self-knowledge preceding order, much of Book X also deals with Satan's return to Hell, where he is greeted by his fallen angels transformed into serpents. Satan's failure to acknowledge his flaws results in his forces being reduced to the lowest level of creation, to serpents, which are now 'accurst/Above all cattle' because of their part in the Fall of man.

I hope by now you will have seen how the text does support a broader political interpretation, and that the modern reader can appreciate the value of *Paradise Lost* as something other than a great religious epic. I would repeat my point that this is *an* interpretation, and that many more passages of a similar nature would need to be examined to support this or any other interpretation. The poem was composed by a profound political thinker and activist, who was clearly attempting to put the history of his own time into the perspective of the Christian vision of God's purpose for humanity. A reading such as I have offered in this chapter approaches that task directly, confronting the layers of meaning, examining the metaphorical and implicit suggestions that appear. It does not 'damage' one's understanding of the text to do this, but widens it, using the approach outlined in this book as a method of entry into a poem that has much to offer the reader, whatever the reason for that reading.

II   Final thoughts on *Paradise Lost*

What else does *Paradise Lost* have to offer? Douglas Bush, in introducing the poem in his Oxford edition of 1966, ends with the following sentence,

> If [the reader's] imagination cannot go along with Milton's passionate faith in God and free will and the attainment of a 'paradise within', he can at least hardly fail to respond to a compassionate myth of the precarious human situation, a myth which in one way or another comprehends all that mankind has felt and done throughout the course of history.   (p. 208)

In other words, the poem has something to offer everyone. To the committed Christian it offers an affirmation of faith, or a source for debate that will deepen his or her understanding. To the historian it offers a wealth of information on seventeenth-century ideas and processes. To the atheist it is an astonishing piece of creative mythology which so humanises the Genesis story that we may end up half-convinced that this was the way things *should* have been. To the student of literature it offers a vocabulary, a wealth of allusion, a use of language that may be beyond comparison, certainly in the field of poetry. To the 'common reader' it is an exciting, well-told, gripping adventure story, that, like a film we have seen many times, continually delights with new-found sources of pleasure. It is almost tragic that the poem belongs to the realms of what we call 'great literature', because that often deters those readers who have perhaps most to gain from reading it. A number of students of mine have asked me to recommend a single literary work and, without hesitation, *Paradise Lost* is my choice. They often feel this is eccentric or perverse, but if they take my advice they return overwhelmed with the experience. Since the early nineteenth century, extended reading has usually meant prose, and the mere idea of reading some two hundred and fifty pages of verse can be off-putting. For those who have not tried it, it is a pleasure that awaits them always.

If you are reading this section looking for advice on approaching other parts of the poem, I would suggest you read Books XI and XII, most of which contain the archangel Michael's account of world history as told to Adam before his expulsion from Paradise. It may not be very accurate historically, even from a seventeenth-century perspective, but it is a masterpiece of selection and story-telling, which finally establishes the central concern of the whole poem that God *has* planned creation, from beginning to end, and that everything and every creature has its rightful place within that plan. Reject the premise if you wish, the account remains fascinating and revealing. Alternatively, read Books V and VI in which another archangel, Raphael, tells Adam all about Satan and his revolt in Heaven. Again, the account may be pure fiction, but the descriptions of the war in Heaven and the preparations for it are without parallel, terrifying and awe-inspiring, and, I would imagine, paradoxically one of the finest pieces of anti-war literature in the English language. The description of the fallen angels, trapped between the forces of God and the abyss beyond Heaven sends a shiver down the spine:

> The monstrous sight
> Strook them with horror backward, but far worse
> Urged them behind; headlong themselves they threw
> Down from the verge of heav'n, eternal wrath
> Burnt after them to the bottomless pit.
>
> (Book VI, ll. 862–6)

However, Milton wrote much else apart from this poem. In the next chapter I am going to look at what are known generally as Milton's 'shorter poems', principally by means of an examination of the elegy *Lycidas* and the court masque *Comus*.

6

The Shorter Poems

Milton is best known for his epic poem, *Paradise Lost*. However, his reputation does not only rest upon this, nor upon the other late pieces, *Paradise Regained* and *Samson Agonistes*. A glance at the list of contents of a complete collection of Milton's poetry will reveal a large number of other poems, many written in languages other than English. In an introduction to Milton's writing such as this is, there is no room to examine more than one or two of the shorter poems, using the method of approach described in previous chapters which can be applied equally well to these. The principal advantage of the shorter poems is that they may be read in their entirety, and that we may thus gather an impression of the whole composition, rather than a fragment of it, as has been the case with *Paradise Lost*. It is interesting to note that many of the oppositions we have traced in that poem are also present in the shorter poems, which indicates that Milton's preoccupations as a poet did not change radically throughout his career. Written prior to the revolution itself, the shorter poems also reveal a writer searching for justification for a number of ideas which may appear, on the surface, to be harsh and restrictive. They frequently concern themselves with questions of morality and 'right-living' which may have been out of favour in the world in which they were written, or may have been distorted by excessively puritanical thinking.

One of the most interesting aspects of these pieces is their variety. Milton, rarely if ever, repeated a particular verse form (with the exception of the sonnet, a form that he frequently 'adapted', nevertheless), writing instead examples of a multitude of classical forms, manipulating each as he felt necessary in order to express his ideas. The two pieces I shall be examining in this chapter are typical of this variety of approach. They were both written within a number of years, *Comus* in or around 1634, and *Lycidas* slightly later in 1637. I shall deal with these two pieces in reverse order of composition mainly because *Lycidas* is much shorter than *Comus* and provides a better route into this group of poems.

Lycidas

I   *Constructing an overall analysis*

Lycidas was written in November 1637, probably at the request of a number of the Fellows of Christ's College, Cambridge, from which Milton had graduated in 1632. It is an elegy, commemorating the death of another student of Christ's, Edward King, who was drowned while on a visit to his home in Ireland. That much can be gathered from the prefatory note which was added to the poem when it was published in a collection of Milton's verse in 1645. A cursory reading of the poem, while making it fairly obvious that this is a poem about someone who has died at sea, may well confuse the modern student, however, in that it refers to Lycidas, who appears to have been a shepherd. What has this to do with Milton, or with a young Cambridge graduate in the early years of the seventeenth century? The straightforward answer is that the poem is written in the form of a 'pastoral elegy', drawing on many previous examples of this, dating back to the classical Greek and Roman poets. Unfortunately, of course, this does not necessarily render much assistance to the student, who is often led off into rather abstruse advice about Virgil and Theocritus by well-meaning but confusing editors. I have drawn your attention to the idea of 'pastoral' writing on one or two occasions in the discussions of *Paradise Lost* (see Chapters 1 and 4), but those points may not be too much help in the present situation.

Let us approach the problem from a slightly different perspective. We know, since the poet tells us, that this is a poem in which 'the Author bewails a learned Friend, unfortunately drowned in his passage from Chester on the Irish Seas'. That man, the 'Friend', was not and never would have been, a 'shepherd' in the strict sense of that word, a man out in the fields protecting sheep. However, your editorial notes may reveal that Edward King either had taken or was preparing for 'holy orders', in other words, he was training to become a minister of the church. In the light of this knowledge, the idea of the man being described as a 'shepherd' begins to take on some meaning, at least in a metaphorical sense, as we are probably aware of the notion of Christ being the 'good shepherd', and of his priests being similarly considered. That, at least, gives us an entry into the poem without becoming embroiled, at this stage, with the meaning and history of 'pastoral' writing. That may come later; first we need to make sense of the poem itself. Now, if the main figure in the poem is described by means of a metaphor, then it seems likely that much else may be equally treated. Be careful here. As with *Paradise Lost*, it is very easy to make the next step turning the poem into an allegory, in which everything represents something else, either more or less exactly. We need not do that; we may accept the metaphorical dimension as a key to our understanding of the poem without insisting that it is in fact about something entirely different. Keeping these thoughts in mind, let us move on.

1   *After reading the text, think about the story and what kind of pattern you can see in it*

As you should have noticed from your preliminary reading, the poem is divided into fairly short verse paragraphs. In my text, there are eleven of these, one or two of which are longer than the others. Let me summarise them briefly:

1.   An introduction. The writer returns to poetry (seen in the metaphor of laurels and myrtles) because Lycidas has died young and must be lamented.
2.   He calls upon the muses to begin his poem, hoping that some other poet may write a similar elegy for himself when he dies.
3.   The poet describes his days with his dead friend, as though they were both shepherds guarding their flocks.
4.   Everything has changed after his death, particularly the natural world where he used to live.
5.   The poet asks why the water nymphs had not protected Lycidas, but realises that they could have done nothing – even Orpheus (an example for the great poet) was allowed to die a horrible death.
6.   He wonders why young men bother to write poetry; and answers himself by saying that they do it for 'fame', which is confirmed by Phoebus.

7.   Returning to the dead man, the poet wonders why he was doomed to such a death, even though the sea was apparently calm, suggesting that the ship was at fault.

8.   A longer paragraph in which Camus (representing Cambridge) mourns the loss of Lycidas, followed by 'The Pilot of the Galilean Lake' (that is, Christ) who regrets the death of Lycidas when many grotesque creatures are allowed to carry on living. These shall soon be disposed of.

9.   The longest paragraph, in contrast to the previous one, describes a funeral cortege on which a long list of flowers is thrown, but this is shown to be a 'false surmise', an illusion, as the body of the dead man has not been recovered from the sea.

10.   Here the poet calls upon other shepherds *not* to lament for Lycidas. Although he is dead he has now gone to Heaven, because of Christ, and will become a guiding spirit for people who travel by sea.

11.   A conclusion appears to shift the narrative voice to an 'uncouth swain', who spends the rest of the day composing further poetry before leaving for somewhere new.

What strikes me immediately when I read this summary is how *little* of the poem actually appears to be devoted to the dead man. He is mentioned in the first paragraph, referred to in paragraph three as a companion of the writer, and apart from indirect references, does not really 'reappear' until paragraph ten. Rather than an elegy to an individual, as we might perhaps expect, the poem appears to concern itself with the writer's own preoccupations, many of which relate to a fear of death before he has achieved 'fame' in this world. The Christian affirmation of life after death in the tenth paragraph seems a curiously tenuous affair, almost 'tagged-on' by necessity rather than conviction. This is particularly so after the volume of references to classical, mythological figures in the previous paragraphs. Also, the final paragraph, with its sudden introduction of a 'narrator', unseen and unexpected until this point, further shifts the poem away from the 'personal' level of a poet writing directly about a dead colleague.

Lycidas, then, appears to have very little to do with the figure named in the title, and even less to do with the man this figure is intended to represent. The central opposition, I would say, is between the chaos of actuality, particularly that of death, and the order of imposed, structured, planned careers. How many of us carefully plot our lives, developing our education and qualifications along certain lines, entering into careers which have controlled channels available for furthering our abilities and talents? At the back of our minds there is always the threat of the anarchy of existence – I could get run over by a bus tomorrow, to quote the old cliche. *Lycidas* is a powerful exploration of that opposition, the tension that propels us forward, sometimes assisted by the promise of eternal life offered by religious belief. The poem is an exercise in self-exploration, using the vehicle of an elegy for a dead poet to explore the tensions felt by the poet himself in his career as a writer. This makes the poem much more interesting to a modern reader, making it accessible as a series of thoughts about the nature of life itself, the way in which individuals order their lives, and the ways in which the chaos of existence often interrupts or undermines that ordering.

Let us look at a few passages in more detail in order to develop this reading.

2   *Select a short passage for discussion and try to build upon the ideas you have established so far*

I shall begin with the opening paragraph:

> Yet once more, O ye laurels, and once more,
> Ye myrtles brown, with ivy never sere,
> I come to pluck your berries harsh and crude,
> And with forced fingers rude
> Shatter your leaves before the mellowing year.
> Bitter constraint, and sad occasion dear,
> Compels me to disturb your season due;
> For Lycidas is dead, dead ere his prime,
> Young Lycidas, and hath not left his peer.
> Who would not sing for Lycidas? He knew
> Himself to sing, and build the lofty rhyme.
> He must not float upon his wat'ry bier
> Unwept, and welter to the parching wind,
> Without the meed of some melodious tear.

> (*Lycidas*, ll. 1–14)

The poem begins with a rather elevated address to the 'laurels' and the 'myrtles', which the 'I' of the poem is going to have to plunder for a funeral wreath because Lycidas is dead. This figure would be lamented by anyone because of his abilities, particularly as a poet, and he cannot be left to die 'unwept'.

The central tension in this passage arises from the violence of the language, particularly in the first half. The reader might expect a poem lamenting the death of a friend to be written in comforting or sad tones; there might be violence in the reaction, when the poet realises the futility of this young death, but surely that would come later. The initial response would be regret. However, *Lycidas* begins with a violent burst of energy, which is not directed at death itself, but at the fact that this young man's death has disrupted the order of things. The arrangement of words in the first two lines emphasises the phrase 'once more', immediately suggesting that this is to be a tedious task, rather than a celebratory or lamentative one. The first sentence itself closes with a series of violent verbs and adjectives – 'harsh and crude', 'forc'd fingers rude', 'shatter your leaves'. This indicates a tone of anger and impatience, of being forced to do something particularly distasteful, and there is also the suggestion that as a result of the imposition of this task, it will not be done very well, because the fingers are 'rude' and they will 'shatter' rather than 'pluck' the leaves. The final phrase 'before the mellowing year' begins to hint at the opposition we are seeking in that it suggests that there *will* come a time when poetry will be written, but later, much later. The violence of the language, the sense of disruption to a planned order which it conveys, all point to a feeling of disquiet and impatience at this interruption to the poet's life.

It may be that the poet opens his elegy with this kind of frustrated, explosive outburst against having actually to write it because he knows that he must do it despite the sadness he feels at the loss of a friend. Yet this poem is clearly something other than a lament for a dead colleague. The opposition which I indicated initially appears to be much closer to the poet's design. He explores the nature of order and chaos, springing as it does from this particular example of the way in which the disorder of death can so easily disrupt the career that an individual plans for himself. Let us now move on into the poem to further this line of thought.

3   *Select a second passage for discussion*

This is the sixth paragraph, which occurs at the mid-point of the poem:

> Alas! what boots it with uncessant care
> To tend the homely slighted shepherd's trade,
> And strictly meditate the thankless Muse?
> Were it not better done as others use,
> To sport with Amaryllis in the shade,
> Or with the tangles of Neaera's hair?
> Fame is the spur that the clear spirit doth raise
> (That last infirmity of noble mind)
> To scorn delights, and live laborious days;
> But the fair guerdon when we hope to find,
> And think to burst out into sudden blaze,
> Comes the blind Fury with th' abhorred shears,
> And slits the thin-spun life. 'But not the praise,'
> Phoebus replied, and touched my trembling ears:
> 'Fame is no plant that grows on mortal soil,
> Nor in the glistering foil
> Set off to th' world, nor in broad rumour lies,
> But lives and spreads aloft by those pure eyes
> And perfect witness of all-judging Jove;
> As he pronounces lastly on each deed,
> Of so much fame in heav'n expect thy meed.'
>
> (*Lycidas*, ll. 64–84)

The writer wonders if there is much point in becoming a poet. It might be better to spend one's time in other pursuits, such as the company of women. The one thing that drives him on is the desire for fame, although the possibility of achieving this may be interrupted by an untimely death. Phoebus responds to the poet's despair by telling him that Jove is the ultimate judge of true fame, and that fame in heaven will be the true poet's reward. There is a break in this paragraph because the speech by Phoebus contrasts quite strongly with the lines which precede it.

The tension in this passage is that of a poet who seems frustrated by the fact that poetry is an apparently thankless task, with the only reward being fame, which is not guaranteed. In the opinion of the poet, his craft is clearly not intended to be 'enjoyable', since it demands a tremendous amount of hard work for very little actual recompense. When the god of poetry tells him that fame is in fact a reward to be given only in heaven this seems implicitly only to aggravate the situation. What underlies the meaning of this passage is the continued notion of the problems presented by the poet's chosen career. He appears to be suggesting that this 'vocation' to which he has devoted his life is a fragile thing, which could be cut off by the randomness of death, so really what is the point in pursuing it. Again, the Christian response, though couched in terms of classical mythology here, is that he should be patient, continue with his work, and receive his reward in due course, after his death. For a young man, conscious of the world's pleasures which he is denying himself in order to develop his career, this does not appear to be a very welcoming prospect. The possibility of premature death, offered by the subject of the elegy, only serves to heighten his doubts. Again, then, the issue of order and chaos is highlighted and this is seen clearly in the language.

The opening sentence of the passage begins the questioning. The 'shepherd's trade' here seems to be a metaphor for poetry, but the adjectives applied to this are disturbing – 'homely slighted'. The first suggests that this is not a particularly adventurous thing to become involved with, and there is a secondary meaning, associating 'homely' with 'ugly' or 'plain' in opposition to 'beautiful', which further suggests the discomfort the poet feels for this occupation. 'Slighted' suggests that poetry is neglected and shunned by most people – a common enough complaint in nearly every age – which again stresses the pointlessness of pursuing it. Similarly, the Muse is described as 'thankless' – there is no direct reward for writing poetry. It is not only these points, however. There is also the fact that the question refers to the need to apply 'uncessant care' to the study of poetry and 'strictly meditate' in order to benefit from it. The ideas bound into this opening sentence remind us of the violence of the first lines of the poem, when the writer seemed impatient at having to write the elegy. Now he seems to be losing patience with his chosen career, which suggests that the disruption of premature death has not only interrupted his studies, but also served to cast doubt on the point of these studies in the first place.

The seventh line of the passage appears at first to show more conviction. What drives the poet on is 'fame' – this is the single force that can sanction the loss of 'delights' and the need for 'laborious days'. However, the note of conviction is quickly dashed when the second half of the sentence introduces the possibility of an early death destroying hopes of worldly fame. The tension in the present passage is the burning desire to achieve fame for oneself, not by means of the work of another. The closing lines of this sentence return to the violent language of the opening. What should be one of the 'Fates' in classical mythology is transposed into a 'blind Fury', a much more bitter description, and her task, to cut the thread of life, is performed with 'abhorred shears', a phrase that continues the shepherd metaphor. Moreover, the life itself, described as 'thin-spun', is said to be 'slit' by these shears, a word which I find particularly harrowing, with all its connotations of finality and yet simplicity. One thinks, perhaps, of someone's throat being 'slit', a very disturbing image which emphasises the destructive, chaotic effect of death.

The response to this offered by Phoebus is altogether more sage and serious, but, almost as a result of this, it seems somehow unconvincing. The god informs the poet that fame is not a worldly achievement, but a reward to be given in heaven. It is interesting to note that the whole speech seems to be delivered to a writer who has been anticipating fame in this world, although that was never made explicit in the previous lines. Put into the mouth of a figure assumed to have greater knowledge, the advice is clearly intended to be unquestionable, but my reading of it is much more as a kind of half-recognition on the writer's part that even fame, the driving force of his career, cannot be achieved by the mortal poet. That distancing effect, together with the too-serious tone of the speech, modifies its effect on the reader, who is thus thrown into sympathy with the poet.

There is little more to be gleaned from this passage. The poet is clearly frustrated by the tenuousness of existence when he has carefully tried to shut himself away in order to achieve a purpose in his life which he is convinced is valid, although he is increasingly doubtful of what it might bring him. Although he proposes fame as his central motivation, what he seems more concerned with is certainty, and that is an aspect of life which is extremely doubtful, paradoxically. There is little point in trying to establish order if nothing can be certain, and, increasingly, the disruptive power of chaos presses in.

4   Select a third passage for discussion

I am going to close this examination of *Lycidas* by looking briefly at the final paragraph, with its disturbing change of 'voice':

> Thus sang the uncouth swain to th' oaks and rills,
> While the still morn went out with sandals grey;
> He touched the tender stops of various quills,
> With eager thought warbling his Doric lay.
> And now the sun had stretched out all the hills,
> And now was dropped into the western bay;
> At last he rose, and twitched his mantle blue:
> Tomorrow to fresh woods, and pastures new.
>
> (*Lycidas*, ll. 186–93)

As we have seen, this passage introduces the 'uncouth swain' who has apparently spoken or sung the previous one hundred and eighty-five lines of the poem. It places this figure in the pastoral landscape of the poem, sets him in a particular time of day – 'the Morn' – and then watches him as the whole day passes and eventually, as evening falls, he leaves. Who is this figure? What is the point of introducing him here, and what purpose is there in placing him so carefully in this temporal setting?

The principal effect of the passage is one of disruption. Throughout the poem we have been considering the 'I' as the poet himself, and by extension, therefore, Milton. I have avoided that last gesture in my discussions but it does tend to be implicit. Now, suddenly, we are informed that our assumptions have been wrong, that the 'I' is not 'the poet', but another poet, who is now being described by what we have presumed is the author. The first result of this disruption to our expectations is to increase the distance between the author and the subject of the poem, Lycidas, or Edward King. This is no longer a personal elegy, but an account of someone else's personal elegy, a someone else who is anonymous and absent. How does this add to our understanding of the whole poem?

I think what it tends to do is give rise to the suggestion that the poem has not been quite such a disruption to the poet's planned existence as we first thought, or even, perhaps, as *he* first thought. By making it explicit that these are someone else's words and thoughts, the poet is able to excuse this interruption as merely an exercise in recording, rather than in actually writing a poem. The irony we recognise is that this is an illusion, the poet *has* written the piece, they *are* his thoughts, but by interposing this anonymous 'author' in the closing lines of his poem he is able to suggest that this is not the case.

The details of the passage support this distancing quite effectively. The poet is described as an 'uncouth swain', an untutored, even possibly ignorant figure who may be excused for writing some of the 'weaker' lines of the poem, as well as for the outbursts against established religion in the eighth paragraph. By implication the true author establishes himself as something other than 'uncouth'. This is not an example of his own writing, but of some other poet whose self-knowledge is far more limited. Equally, the 'swain' appears to have no audience other than the natural elements such as trees and water – 'oaks and rills' – and surely there is no fame to be had from writing for these. The careful placing of the poem as being sung in the morning refers us back to the disruption to due season that we saw in the opening lines, but it also confirms, metaphorically, the fact that this is an early work by the poet-swain – his later work, presumably, will be much better. We cannot help but interpret this as a reference to the true poet, who is further excusing his own weaknesses at this early point in his career as a poet. Finally, the much-quoted last two lines of the poem complete the distancing effect that has been present throughout. Tomorrow will bring new ideas, new forms, new thoughts. These recorded here are passing thoughts, valid for a short period but soon to be superseded by newer and fresher ones.

By the end of this paragraph, the illusion of the 'poet-swain' and the 'true poet' as separate existences is almost extinguished, and we are enabled to read back into the poem in the way we did at the beginning. The poet has re-established the order of his own career, dispelled the fears that were aroused by learning of the premature death of Lycidas, and can now look forward again to new experiences which will occur in an assured future that begins 'tomorrow'. I have always found the word 'twitch'd' in the last but one line to be particularly significant. It is curiously comic in a strange way, as it suggests only the slightest of movements, implying that the apparent depth of feeling recorded in the poem is really only a simple, passing fancy that is easily discarded in the light of a much more certain route into a greater future. Needing no more than the slightest adjustment, the poet's 'mantle' is returned to its correct position, and he sets off on his course again. The apparent fears that were provoked by the thoughts of premature death have been removed by the recognition that we cannot allow the chaos of death to long disrupt the planned order of our lives. As far as we know, there will be a tomorrow, we can plan for it, and the problem of death, particularly for a young person, can simply be shrugged off as occasionally worrying, but not of any long term concern.

II Aspects of the poem

My reading of the poem attempts to make it accessible to a modern audience because it allows us to see the ways in which the young Milton was coming to terms with his own 'vocation' as a poet. It stops the poem being simply a rather dry elegy for some unknown figure in the early seventeenth century, which on one level it is, by adding the much more significant point that it has a broader thematic interest.

The idea I have put forward is that the poem is a young man's exploration of the problems that can be caused to an ordered, planned life when a colleague's premature death gives rise to fears that this may be something that could happen to us all. Fear of death is a perfectly natural thing, as long as it is not allowed to rule our lives. Some kind of religious belief may bring comfort to those who have these fears, but this does not necessarily dispel the fear itself. *Lycidas*, in the final analysis, stresses that these fears are momentary and passing – we are right to have them, but they must be seen as part of the greater pattern of human existence, rather than as the incursion of chaos into an individual's life. If we are to achieve something as individuals we need to plan and order our lives, accepting that there are forces which may terminally disrupt those plans, but not rejecting the order outright because of them.

Knowing these things also helps the reader to understand the classical references embedded in the poem. They achieve a sense of distance and imply an idea of artistic order and tradition which serves further to counter the potential chaos of premature death. They are aspects of a poet's career that he may set against the feelings of pain and loss over the death of a friend because they add a necessary understanding of poise, continuity and a knowledge that although the natural order has been interrupted, it will inevitably return. This underlying contrast between the actual death and classical models of poetic handling of death helps to strengthen and shape the whole poem.

Comus

I   Constructing an overall analysis

When we turn to *Comus*, we arrive for the first time in this book at a full-blown dramatic piece of writing. In my examination of *Paradise Lost* I frequently referred to its dramatic qualities, particularly as the central figures in that poem emerged and reacted with each other. *Comus*, though, is a true drama, spoken by a cast of characters with no narrative interruption or links. It was intended for performance, and was indeed performed shortly after Milton wrote it, but it belongs to a curious and fairly short-lived literary genre known as the 'masque'. This is a sort of elaborate melodrama using classical figures as the cast. What makes *Comus* interesting is the way in which it explores, through this medium, issues of chastity and male aggression. I prefer to look at the piece as a 'dramatic poem' in that it is a series of highly structured set speeches within a dramatic framework.

The other problem that may strike the new reader is the use of classical figures and allusions, similar to that we have just encountered with *Lycidas*. On first reading, the whole thing can appear desperately artificial and static, full of long speeches using a fairly elevated tone and vocabulary, apparently all about some vague notion of 'virtue' and, presumably, 'vice'. The stage directions, such as they are, seem absurd and fanciful, containing phrases such as 'with him a rout of monsters, headed like sundry sorts of wild beasts', or 'soft music, tables spread with all dainties'. We may be captivated by one or two passages of effective writing, but our overall impression is of a somewhat tedious, airy-fairy 'poetic' thing that is not in the least appealing. We turn to the critics for help, only to be told of its high moral content, an examination of the conflict between a young virtuous maiden and a rather nasty character who tries to tempt her in some way, until she is rescued by a river goddess. This is, then, a 'pastoral drama', and our hearts sink at the re-appearance of that word, synonymous with tedium and the dullest kind of 'poetry'. In common with the other parts of this book, my task here is to enter into the text itself to see what it actually has to offer. Once again, I would suggest you pick up your text and read it through *without* reference to notes and introductions.

1   *After reading the text, think about the story and what kind of pattern you can see it*

Let's start, as usual, with a fairly thorough summary.

The poem opens with a 92 line introduction spoken by the Attendant Spirit. This figure introduces himself as a kind of 'guardian angel' whose job is to protect virtuous human beings when they are in danger. He sets the scene as being on the borders of Wales, at present ruled over by a 'noble Peer', whose sons and daughters are coming to join him. Their journey lies through a dark wood, which is endangered by the presence of Comus, the son of Circe and Bacchus, who has the ability to turn travellers into animals who then become part of his entourage. The Spirit is here to bring protection to the peer's children in the guise of a young shepherd. As Comus and his band enter, he becomes invisible.

   Comus enters with his band of transformed humans. He tells us it is evening and the time for 'Midnight shout and revelry' to begin. Much of this revelry is to do with a kind of drunken debauchery as Comus praises the night. The creatures begin to dance. Suddenly Comus tells them to stop as he has heard one of the children approaching. He disguises his band and, by means of charms, turns the place into a comforting spot and himself into 'some harmless villager'. As he has predicted, the daughter, called the 'Lady', enters.

   The Lady cannot understand how the sounds of the 'ill-manag'd merriment' she thought she heard have disappeared. She tells us that she has become lost in the forest after her brothers had left her, apparently sleeping, to find some food. Since they appeared not to have returned, she has set off in search of them, but is now lost. She is worried about the noises she thinks she heard, but she reassures herself that she will be protected by a 'glistering guardian' because of her virtue, principally her Chastity. She sings a song in case her brothers are near enough to hear her. Comus, entranced by her singing, is much taken by the Lady and speaks to her. The Lady, thinking he is a 'gentle shepherd', rejects his exaggerated praise and asks if he can help her find her brothers. Comus questions her closely as to why she is here and how old her brothers are. He pretends to have seen them further off and offers to take her to them. He assures her he can find the way in the dark, and, if not, he will take her to 'a low/But loyal cottage' for the night. She trusts his word and goes with him.

The two brothers enter. They are perplexed by the darkness of the wood, and the younger brother is concerned for the plight of their sister. The elder brother assures him that she will be safe because there is no danger, and, anyway, she will be protected by her own virtue. The younger brother agrees to this but still insists that some unknown danger might happen to her. The elder suggests that he is conscious of the danger but inclined to reject it since their sister has 'a hidden strength'. When the younger asks what this is, he tells him that it is her chastity, an attribute he expands upon at length, which reassures him somewhat. They hear someone coming and take up defensive positions, but it turns out to be the Attendant Spirit, disguised as their father's shepherd, Thyrsis. Asking for the Lady, they tell him she is lost. The Spirit tells them about the dangers presented by Comus and his band of transformed humans. He has heard them earlier as they revelled in the wood, and then how the noise suddenly stopped. He heard the singing and recognised the voice as their sister's, and then pursued the Lady, but found her talking to Comus. Hearing her story he has come in search of the brothers. The younger brother accuses the elder of misleading him, but the latter insists that their sister's virtue will protect her until they can find her. The Spirit tells him he is powerless against Comus's charms, but he is protected by a magical potion called Haemony which he will give to them. When they attack Comus they must be sure to seize his magic wand.

The scene changes to Comus's palace, where the Lady is trapped in 'an enchanted chair'. Comus threatens the Lady that he will turn her to stone, but she rejects his threats by asserting her mental freedom. He tries to persuade her that her chastity is unnatural, and that she is misusing the attributes she has been given. She accuses him of having lied to her and rejects his offer of the drink that will turn her into one of his followers. Comus retorts that her claims to have a 'well-govern'd and wise appetite' are equally unnatural, as temperance would lead to the world being swamped with the benefits Nature has to offer. Her chastity will only lead to her becoming an ugly old maid. The Lady responds to this by telling him that Nature can govern herself, and that all her goods are given only to those who may best use them. Recognising the pointlessness of trying to reason with him, she tells him that the strength of her virtue will overcome him in the end. Comus then attempts to force her to drink.

The brothers burst in, smash the cup holding the drink, and capture Comus's band. The Spirit laments that they have allowed Comus to escape by not breaking his wand, which means that they cannot release their sister. He remembers that the goddess of the local river, Sabrina, who had once been in a similar position, might be able to help them, and he summons her by means of a song. He is successful, Sabrina arrives, agrees to help the Lady, releases her, and then returns to the river. The Spirit thanks Sabrina and leaves the wood with the children, taking them to their 'Father's residence' in Ludlow.

The final scene sees the children restored to their parents, and in an 'epilogue' the Spirit tells how he will return to 'the broad fields of the sky' now his task is completed. He ends with an assertion that Virtue is the route by which humans may reach heaven.

Now, I recognise that this is a lengthy summary, but it does have a purpose. In this simplified, prose account of the poem, we are not immediately confused or put off by the myriad allusions or classical references that can clog the new reader's understanding. The poem is seen to have a fairly straightforward 'story' in which Good triumphs over Evil in a resounding fashion, and in which none of the main protagonists is seen to suffer any long-lasting harm. That, however, tends to leave us feeling rather disappointed. My initial reaction to this might well be, 'So what?' A rather clichéd idea, wrapped up in a fairly original format, but nevertheless rather dull and unexciting. Can there be any more to this piece? Obviously, the answer has to be, yes, but if so, what?

Let us look through the summary to see if there are any interesting oppositions that appear, apart from the rather too obvious good and evil, although we should note at this stage the continuation of this opposition in Milton's poetry. What first strikes me is the amazing independence of the Lady. She appears alone at first, is taken in easily by the disguised Comus, but then resists him by strength of argument, physical resistance being literally impossible. Then there is the curious vacillation of the brothers, the elder of whom seems willing at first to believe that there is no danger, then that the sister's chastity is defence enough, while the younger, by contrast, imagines all sorts of things happening to her. When danger appears to confront them, however, they become immediately, and physically, defensive. Finally, there is the inability of the brothers, or the Attendant Spirit, to release the Lady from her imprisonment. This can only be achieved by *another* female figure, Sabrina. The opposition that is building itself here is between male and female, but more subtly than that, between the reader's perception of the strengths and weaknesses of male and female, in particular perhaps, as regards masculine attitudes towards female strengths and weaknesses, and the actuality of these. You may be beginning to think that this is something of a feminist angle to take on the poem, and I would admit that, in twentieth-century terms, that may be so. Nevertheless, this is an opposition which would be worth exploring because it adds a new dimension to the interest of the poem, appearing, as it does, to suggest that Milton was concerned for the position of women in society in a way that critics, particularly of *Paradise Lost*, with its apparent contempt for women in the figure of Eve, have rarely been able to see.

My overall impression of *Comus* is of a poem that presents a woman perfectly in control of herself, confronted with the masculine world in its two most typical forms – one, the lusting, bestial figure whose sole idea of sexual intercourse is rape; the other, the over-protective, shielding figure who hides his women away from others but is useless when they are left unguarded. It is always something of a disappointment to me, whenever I read the poem, to come upon the stage direction which brings in the two brothers at the climax of Comus's assault on their sister. I am convinced that she would have successfully rebutted Comus, even in his physical assault, had they not appeared, and, in the end, the villain of the piece escapes scot-free, presumably to pursue his lustful desires on some other 'poor, unsuspecting female'. But that, of course, is rather useless 'what if' speculation!

I shall examine a few passages in detail to see how far the opposition I have noted may be substantiated.

2 *Select a short passage for discussion and try to build upon the ideas you have established so far*

I shall begin with a few lines taken from the Attendant Spirit's introduction:

> And all this tract that fronts the falling sun
> A noble peer of mickle trust and power
> Has in his charge, with tempered awe to guide
> An old and haughty nation proud in arms;
> Where his fair offspring, nursed in princely lore,
> Are coming to attend their father's state
> And new-entrusted sceptre; but their way
> Lies through the perplexed paths of this drear wood,
> The nodding horror of whose shady brows
> Threats the forlorn and wand'ring passenger.
> And here their tender age might suffer peril,
> But that by quick command from soveran Jove
> I was despatched for their defence and guard;
> And listen why, for I will tell ye now
> What never yet was heard in tale or song
> From old or modern bard in hall or bow'r.
>
> (*Comus*, ll. 30–45)

This passage is just a part of the verse paragraph in which the Spirit is 'setting the scene'. In particular he is placing the action in the part of the country presently ruled over by a Peer who was, as your notes will probably inform you, John Egerton, Earl of Bridgewater, at the time Lord President of the Council of Wales and its Marches. The rest we already know from the earlier summary of the whole poem.

The particular tension which arises in this passage results from the position of the father, as 'ruler' of a large tract of land, and the situation we find his own children in, following 'the perplex'd paths of [a] drear wood' in order to reach him. The opposition is immediately one between protection and actuality. Here we have this figure whose role is to act as 'guide' to 'An old and haughty nation', which he 'Has in his charge', yet at the same time the only route his own children have to reach him is through this wood, with its 'nodding horror' which 'Threats the forlorn and wand'ring passenger'. This uncomfortable tension undermines both the protective role of the Peer, as regards the country he rules over, and the quality of that protection if he is incapable of guarding his own family. What is the text suggesting here?

The first sentence appears to be straightforward enough, complimenting not only the Peer himself, but also the country which he has in his charge, and the children. On the surface at least, this does not seem to be one of Milton's open attacks on government by the aristocracy, which is perhaps inevitable given that *Comus* was written for aristocrats. However, there are one or two little oddities here. How could a loving father, who appears to have such power, allow his own children to travel such a path and face such obvious danger? The Attendant Spirit immediately lightens the fear by telling us that he has been sent 'for their defence and guard' – but doesn't that only further compound the father's lack of foresight? The Spirit points out that the children are young by reference to 'their tender age', and it is interesting to note that Jove is referred to as 'sovran' which ties back in with the Peer's position. Finally, the passage ends with what, on the surface, might seem to be a fairly innocuous and clichéd statement, that he is about to tell a story that 'never yet was heard'.

There is not much else to be said here. The doubts are sowed in the reader's mind, a questioning of relationships and of the protection that one would expect to be offered by close, family ties. The implications of a text that seems literally to be telling a rather coy little fairy tale are interesting. The passage ties in with the central opposition because of the fact that this questioning relates directly to the father – the masculine figure in a family group who is automatically assumed to be the protector and provider. Here it seems at least doubtful as to the quality of his provision of either of these, and that must cast some doubt upon the masculine elements within the poem. I can say little more than this, at this stage, so I shall move on to find another passage.

3   Select a second passage for discussion

The following lines are taken from Comus's first speech:

> Meanwhile welcome joy and feast,
> Midnight shout and revelry,
> Tipsy dance and jollity.
> Braid your locks with rosy twine
> Dropping odours, dropping wine,
> Rigour now is gone to bed,
> And Advice with scrupulous head,
> Strict Age, and sour Severity,
> With their grave saws in slumber lie.
> We that are of purer fire
> Imitate the starry quire,
> Who in their nightly watchful spheres
> Lead in swift round the months and years.
> The sounds and seas with all their finny drove
> Now to the moon in wavering morris move,
> And on the tawny sands and shelves
> Trip the pert fairies and the dapper elves;
> By dimpled brook and fountain brim
> The wood-nymphs, decked with daisies trim,
> Their merry wakes and pastimes keep:
> What hath night to do with sleep?
> Night hath better sweets to prove,
> Venus now wakes, and wakens Love.
>
> (*Comus*, ll. 102–24)

This passage serves essentially to show that Comus represents the 'bestial' side of man's nature. The text, in both language and structure as well as content, emphasises the decadent, debauched existence that is led by Comus and his band. There are two details of particular interest – the personified abstract moral qualities referred to in the first few lines, and the irony that is strongly present in the closing lines. The intervening section first broaches Comus's idea that the world of nature supports his life-style, an idea that he will return to when in discussion with the Lady.

The opening lines set up their own opposition. Comus's choice of qualities, 'Rigour', 'advice', 'Strict Age' and 'sour severity', reveals that his opinion of the alternative moral life-style he rejects is one of restriction and confinement. The problem, of course, is that he does not set up a strictly objective set of alternatives, and thus his argument is easily won. Implicit in the named qualities are their opposites, so that his lifestyle can be seen to be that of a lax, loose-moraled libertine whose sole excuse for his behaviour might be his youth. The text is establishing Comus as the figure of 'man' in his most unpleasant form, and the closing lines of the passage strengthen this by showing that the end-result of all this laxity and decadence will be sexual gratification for purely animal reasons. The rhetorical question, 'What hath night to do with sleep?' is both a crude double-entendre and an answer to itself, for the response would be either 'nothing' or 'everything'. When Comus suggests that the night 'wakens Love' it is already plain that his definition of that term has little to do with spiritual or moral qualities, but is purely physical – he means 'Lust' rather than 'Love'.

This, then, is the face of masculinity that is not in the least appealing, since it rejects any possible sense of a true relationship for licentious behaviour and crude, physical passion. As the 'villain' of the piece, we might expect Comus to be portrayed in this way, but I think that the important point to note is how far the text itself subtly fogs the true impact by means of the apparently simple, easy references to the natural world. Comus's life-style may be 'natural', but it is to be condemned because it is not ordered and controlled as befits a fully rational human being but is lacking in value, subject only to animal appetites, which you may recall was the problem with Adam and Eve after the Fall in *Paradise Lost.* Let me move on to a further piece.

4   *Select a third passage for discussion*

In order to establish the presence in the text of the 'alternative' type of male figure I shall look briefly at a passage describing the Lady's brothers:

My brothers, when they saw me wearied out
With this long way, resolving here to lodge
Under the spreading favour of these pines,
Stepped as they said to the next thicket side
To bring me berries, or such cooling fruit
As the kind hospitable woods provide.
They left me then when the grey-hooded Ev'n,
Like a sad votarist in palmer's weed,
Rose from the hindmost wheels of Phoebus' wain.
But where they are, and why they came not back,
Is now the labour of my thoughts; 'tis likeliest
They had engaged their wand'ring steps too far,
And envious darkness, ere they could return,
Had stole them from me.

> (*Comus*, ll. 182–95)

The tension here, as the Lady describes her brothers' leaving of her, is in her perception of their role as they understand it, and her much more subtle opinion of that role. The tension is particularly noticeable in the qualifying phrases such as 'as they said', which immediately cast doubt on the true nature of what is being done. The brothers claimed that they were not going far, only to the 'next thicket side', but they promptly disappeared. What sort of protection were they offering their sister, to leave her beneath some trees just as evening is falling? Again, the text stresses that although the brothers appear to have some concern, as they can see she is tired after the journey, nevertheless it is the 'kind hospitable wood' which will provide something for her; they themselves can offer nothing. In the same way as their father, they appear not to have made any preparations for this journey. The Lady attempts to excuse their absence by accusing 'envious darkness' of having 'stole them from me', yet this only gives rise to the thought that they must have been quite unthinking to have wandered off so far in the first place. The impact of this passage is fairly clear, I think. The brothers represent the kind of male figures who superficially profess to be able to protect their womenfolk, but who rarely give any real thought to what this task demands, and frequently in fact expose women to greater dangers by their clumsy mishandling of situations which arise. It is interesting to note that the rest of the Lady's speech shows that she is not really afraid in her present situation, as she is confident in her own ability to protect herself. In fact, by the end of it, just before she starts to sing, she talks of having 'new-enliven'd spirits' – very different indeed from the younger brother's imagining of her possible fate.

Already, then, only some two hundred lines into the poem, it is beginning to become clear that this male/female opposition is powerfully present as an undercurrent driving forward the plot. The passage in which the brothers debate upon their sister's absence serves, as a discussion of values, to further reinforce our vision of them as somewhat helpless, though undoubtedly well-intentioned. I shall move on now to a further speech by the Lady when she is actually confronted by Comus, trapped in the 'enchanted chair' in his 'stately palace'.

5   Select a fourth passage for discussion

This is the end of the Lady's final speech to Comus:

> To him that dares
> Arm his profane tongue with contemptuous words
> Against the sun-clad power of Chastity,
> Fain would I something say, yet to what end?
> Thou hast nor ear nor soul to apprehend
> The sublime notion and high mystery
> That must be uttered to unfold the sage
> And serious doctrine of Virginity,
> And thou art worthy that thou shouldst not know
> More happiness than this thy present lot.
> Enjoy your dear wit and gay rhetoric
> That hath so well been taught her dazzling fence;
> Thou art not fit to hear thyself convinced.
> Yet should I try, the uncontrolled worth
> Of this pure cause would kindle my rapt spirits
> To such a flame of sacred vehemence
> That dumb things would be moved to sympathize,
> And the brute Earth would lend her nerves, and shake,
> Till all thy magic structures, reared so high,
> Were shattered into heaps o'er thy false head.

(*Comus*, ll. 780–99)

This is a powerful and highly-charged condemnation of Comus and all he represents. As a piece of dramatic writing it is equally resonant, as the text moves from question to answer to statement, with various syntactical devices such as repetition and reversal of expected word order. The Lady realises that she should answer Comus's arguments against her chastity, yet she recognises that his base nature would mean her words would be wasted. She ends by affirming that if she *did* try her power would be tremendous.

What is most interesting in the first ten or twelve lines of this passage is the Lady's characterisation of Comus and the type of men he represents. She clearly categorises him as a purely sensual, physical creature with no ability to appreciate what we might call the 'finer qualities' of woman. The tension in this first part of the passage arises from the qualities that she does attribute to Comus, which we might expect to be more akin to a 'spiritual' man, yet which are clearly criticised here. Having said that he is incapable of understanding spiritual matters, she makes the heavily ironic statement that he is 'worthy' that he should 'not know / More happiness than this [his] present lot'. This suggests that Comus is actually incapable of achieving a higher appreciation, but worse than this, that he is satisfied with what he has, believing that this is all he requires. This is a substantial criticism of men who believe that physical enjoyment is all they should aspire to, and clearly raises the position of the Lady, and, by implication, that of women in general. Next she tells him to 'Enjoy [his] dear wit and gay rhetoric' which she compares to the skills of fencing. That metaphor itself is subtle because it associates wit and rhetoric with a sport that is clever, but potentially deadly – fencing, after all, is performed with swords, the purpose of which is to kill other men. It is perhaps the unexpected condemnation of these two aspects, wit and rhetoric, which most surprises the reader. We might anticipate that they would belong to men in the 'higher' realm, but the Lady clearly associates this quality with unthinking, physical men. Worst of all, despite his wit, he cannot be convinced of the wrongness of his position, which condemns him forever. The strength of the tensions in these lines is most prevalent in the apparently positive qualities by which Comus's low nature is condemned. She speaks of him being 'worthy', of having been 'well taught', yet in the end he is 'not fit'. By implication, Comus, and those like him, are condemned for their misapprehension of their condition, but most of all, perhaps, for their misuse of the means by which they may have possibly become better. Comus is an 'educated' figure, but that education has been useless, applied to one incapable of improvement.

By contrast, the Lady's power and self-knowledge comes across well. Central to this is her awareness of the fact that, should she respond as the situation demands, then she would be revealing the 'uncontrolled worth' of what is termed her 'pure cause'. That control is central to the opposition in the whole text. Women are perceived to be creatures subject to the whim or will of men, whether they be brutal and physical like Comus, or over-protective and clumsy like her brothers. The former type has no use for women other than as sexual objects to satisfy their animal lusts, the latter type sees women as porcelain figures best locked in glass cages, out of harm's way, as far as they are concerned. The Lady's hinting at her far greater and potentially more powerful qualities confirms the interest of the text in the true position of woman in society. They may be subject to men, because men are too ignorant to recognise their value, but that subjection, when it exists, is only ever physical, for mentally and spiritually women are much more liberated than men will ever be.

Comus's reaction in the lines following this passage confirms this, when he responds 'She fables not', and admits that he is afraid of the 'power' that she reveals. The Lady is established as a figure of tremendous power, that may be latent and 'controlled' for much of the time, but which could be released with potentially devastating effect. It is interesting to return to the summary and note that Comus's next action is to turn to physical force, and that his attempt to 'rape' the Lady is foiled by the physical force offered by her brothers. Men, in general, in the end resort to the only superior quality they *appear* to possess, which is their physical strength. After the Lady's quiet condemnation of Comus and his arguments, even that is put into doubt.

II Aspects of the poem

Our fairly thorough examination of this aspect of *Comus* has revealed something of the potential the text possesses. As I said in my introductory paragraphs to the poem, the opposition I have sought renders the poem much more accessible to a modern reader, but that does not mean that this was not an aspect of the text in its seventeenth-century context. The position of woman in society was much debated by the religious thinkers of the time, who were trying to find a way forward from the turbulence of the previous century's reformation of the church and its attitudes to the laity. Milton himself, indeed, was fascinated by this question, as a number of his early prose pamphlets indicate, particularly perhaps the tract *On Divorce*, which brought him unsought-for notoriety. In its own way, as we have seen, *Comus* contributes to this debate, presenting a case for the re-examination of the role of woman in society by exploring the nature of men's attitudes to her. By placing his 'heroine' in a situation where she is to be tested severely, Milton has carefully established an argument which shows the strength of womankind in general. Woman's apparent submission and passivity are revealed to disguise latent strengths that contribute far more to a sense of order and control in society than men are willing to admit. The Lady of the poem is a figure of independent strength who, in the end, fights her own battle, unaided by her so-called protectors, and not frightened by the animal lusts of Comus. The only way in which she is actually restrained is by the force of magic, when she is trapped in what the Attendant Spirit describes as 'stony fetters fix'd and motionless'. The power of the petrifying metaphor is that it amplifies the text's condemnation of man's attempts to subjugate the will of woman, to trap her into unthinking, unfeeling positions in society, not allowing true social development to take place in which woman assumes her rightful place as man's equal, if, indeed, not his superior. This tension is ultimately resolved by the actions of Sabrina, who alone is able to release the Lady. This metaphor of what perhaps the modern world might call 'female solidarity' encapsulates the central concern of the text – man is incapable, because of his prejudice and blinkered thinking, of releasing woman from her position, but women, together, may isolate and enfeeble men's strength and thereby gain release. One wonders how the audience of 1634 reacted to these propositions, presented under the guise of a fanciful masque acted out by a group of children.

Other shorter poems

I do not have the space to examine other of Milton's shorter pieces here, but the same method may be applied to your study of them.

I would suggest that you look at those entitled 'On the Morning of Christ's Nativity', 'L'Allegro' and 'Il Penseroso', as good points of entry into Milton's works. You might also look at some of the sonnets, many of which develop these concerns in the way that this form is best able to do, presenting a short but pithy consideration of an often powerful issue. The important point is to concentrate upon the text itself, rather than get entangled in a wealth of textual notes that attempt to 'explain' the poems in some way. Your confidence in handling these texts will grow as you cover more of them, and if the interest and delight is maintained, the opportunity for further exploration will probably present itself in the future. I am now going to move on to the final text in this book, the late dramatic poem *Samson Agonistes*.

7
Samson Agonistes

I Constructing an overall analysis

Samson Agonistes was very probably Milton's last composed poem.
That in itself, however, is something of a controversy, since there is
no evidence to show that it was *written* later than the other poems,
although it was certainly published, together with *Paradise Regained,*
in 1671, some four years after *Paradise Lost.* Certain critical writers
and biographers have attempted to prove that *Samson Agonistes* may
have been written as early as 1647, more than twenty years before
its publication. The arguments for and against early and late dates
of composition are fairly complex and are certainly not particularly
relevant in the present context. Suffice it to say that I tend to accept
the suggestion that it was Milton's last poem, and I will write of it as
though it were.

Once again, as with *Comus,* I shall call the piece a poem, although
strictly speaking it is a 'drama' based on classical models. However,
it is extremely difficult to imagine *Samson Agonistes* being produced
for the stage, and it is doubtful if that was ever the author's intention.
As throughout Milton's career, he is here experimenting with a
new form, which although it is called 'dramatic' remains essentially
a poetic form. This is an important distinction to understand,
because, in my experience, students often come to study *Samson
Agonistes* at the same time as, or shortly after having studied,
Shakespeare, and they obviously find it difficult to come to terms
with a text where nothing *seems* to happen.

As a poetic form, however, *Samson Agonistes* follows very closely
indeed the model laid down by the Greek philosopher Aristotle
in his text on the forms of poetry, which in classical times meant
virtually everything that was written. While I do not intend to refer
to this model in too much detail, it does at least provide a way of
breaking up the text into manageable proportions. The edition that

you are using may already provide this, but in case it does not, here is an outline of *Samson Agonistes* according to Aristotle's plan.

The classical form of *Samson Agonistes*

Section	Lines	Principal Characters
Prologos	1 – 114	Samson
Parode	115 – 175	Chorus
1st Episode	176 – 292	Samson and Chorus
1st Stasimon	293 – 325	Samson, Chorus and Manoa
2nd Episode	326 – 651	Samson and Manoa
2nd Stasimon	652 – 709	Chorus
3rd Episode	710 – 1009	Samson and Dalila
3rd Stasimon	1010 – 1060	Chorus
4th Episode	1061 – 1267	Samson and Harapha
4th Stasimon	1268 – 1296	Chorus
5th Episode	1297 – 1426	Samson and Officer
5th Stasimon	1427 – 1440	Chorus
Exode	1441 – 1659	Manoa and Chorus
Kommos	1660 – 1758	Semi-chorus, Chorus, Manoa

As may be seen from this table, the five 'episodes' are basically equivalent to the five acts of a Shakespearean play, with a prologue and an epilogue and five intervening commentaries by the Chorus. Shakespeare's *Henry V* follows this pattern fairly closely, although that is a much more stage-conscious piece. There are no indications in the text of *Samson Agonistes* that this division is present, but if you summarise the poem, you will find that most of the divisions noted in the table are fairly obvious. My own working summary, which took no notice of the classical model, actually divided the poem into eleven sections, most of which are reflected in the table, except that I read the first three hundred and twenty-five lines (that is the Parode, 1st Episode and 1st Stasimon) as one unit. This gives the reader manageable portions of the text to deal with, as well as giving some insight into the more traditional approaches to this work.

The *content* of *Samson Agonistes*, surprisingly enough, may be fairly easily summarised. Based loosely on the biblical character who is recorded in the Old Testament Book of Judges, the story relates the final hours of the hero figure Samson, who was reputed to have superhuman strength endowed as a gift from God and which was lodged in his hair. He has been duped into revealing this secret by his second wife Dalila, who was a Philistine, one of the enemies of the Hebrew people at this point in their history. She has, in turn, revealed this to the Philistines who have thereby been enabled to capture Samson by shaving his head. Now he is their slave, set to work at a mill in a prison in Gaza, and to cause him further anguish his captors have blinded him. The poem itself covers the last day of his life, a day when he is allowed some respite from his labours as the Philistines are celebrating the feast day of their god, Dagon. Samson is approached, in turn, by his father Manoa, who is seeking some way of releasing him from his captivity; his wife Dalila, who seeks to be reconciled with him; a champion of the Philistines, Harapha, who taunts Samson over his loss of physical powers; and finally by an officer who demands that he present himself at the temple of Dagon in order to entertain the Philistines. Although at first he refuses this demand, Samson eventually submits, is led off, and, we later discover, destroys the temple by pulling down the central pillars, killing himself and large numbers of the Philistine dignitaries present. Because the poem maintains what are known as the classical 'unities' of place, time and action, the final catastrophe takes place offstage and is reported to the 'audience' and those who remained behind by means of a messenger who has witnessed the events. This goes some way towards explaining the apparently static nature of the text. There is little or no physical *action*, beyond the entrances and exits of the main characters, but there is, by contrast, a great deal of moral, political and spiritual debate which provides the main interest of the poem.

What we have here is Milton's finest attempt to create a poem in which the characters themselves provide the main bulk of the material, without the presence of a narrator figure who can manipulate the reader's point of view. The chorus does not provide a narration, but rather acts as a foil to the developing tensions of Samson's encounters with his four protagonists. Central to our enjoyment of the poem is the development of the figure of Samson, who, within the course of the plot, rediscovers himself, comes to terms with his own despairing outlook, re-asserts the validity of his role within God's plan and is thus enabled to perform his last, heroic action. The other figures act as the means by which Samson eventually comes to this rediscovery of self, prompting him to engage with the problems presented by filial responsibility (the relation between son and father), sexual responsibility (the relation between man and wife), temporal, power-seeking responsibility (the relation between the champions of two nations), and finally responsibility to one's people (the reaction of Samson to the demands of the officer). All of these problems are aspects of the 'umbrella' responsibility which is spiritual – the relation between Samson and God. If that appears to be rather complex, it may be simplified into the opposition of the individual and order, one of the central aspects in much of Milton's writing. How does Samson, as the champion of the Hebrew people, come to terms with the devastation of his captivity and degradation and re-assert himself and his beliefs, and thus the position of his people, in the face of apparently overwhelming odds?

The prominence in *Samson Agonistes* of the issue of spiritual responsibility – the relation between God and Man, and Milton's need to justify the ways of God to man – follows on from the concerns and debate which prompted *Paradise Lost*. Samson has to come to terms with the situation he is in, and somehow overturn this, if he is to prove that God's having chosen him amongst all his people was for a purpose. What makes the opposition fascinating in *Samson Agonistes* is that the hero, Samson, is completely and utterly *human*, subject to all the forces that may tempt and pervert a man's career, against which only he himself may struggle. In *Paradise Lost* the central heroic figure is Christ, who is prepared to sacrifice himself in return for the eventual salvation of mankind. This is true also of the later poem *Paradise Regained*, where Christ features more prominently, but in the same role. *Samson Agonistes* provides a human hero, whose actions may provide the final justification of God's ways, without any hint of the divine intervention that is inevitable with the Son of God. It is remarkable that the Samson of the poem does not possess, while 'on stage', those divine powers that God has lodged in his hair, and so he is consistently and dramatically *human*. There is also little recourse to calling upon divine intervention in order to solve his problems. Very early on in the text, Samson recognises that he has brought about his own destruction:

> Nothing of all these evils hath befall'n me
> But justly; I myself have brought them on,
> Sole Author I, sole cause.
>
> (*Samson Agonistes*, ll. 374–6)

Thus he also recognises that it is by reconstructing his own selfhood, through his own endeavours, that he may come to that situation where the chorus and others may:

> of me expect to hear
> Nothing dishonourable, impure, unworthy,
> Our God, our Law, my Nation, or myself.
>
> (*Samson Agonistes*, ll. 1423–5)

Samson Agonistes, then, is the chronicle of a quest for self-discovery, and it is as such that I am going to examine it in a little more detail. There are a number of alternative approaches, some of which are more enticing than others, but I believe that by exploring Samson's journey to the recovery of his selfhood, principally by means of an examination of a number of passages in which the journey is explained, we may come to the beginnings of an appreciation of this very powerful piece of writing.

1   *Select a short passage for discussion and try to build upon the ideas you have established so far*

The poem opens with a lengthy soliloquy by Samson, which initially makes clear where the action of the plot is taking place, and why Samson has been given this opportunity to put aside his labours. After that, the soliloquy is a consistent lament in which Samson 'bemoan[s] his condition', as the Argument puts it. Samson questions the divine prophecies of his birth, the nature of his upbringing, the loss of his strength, and, most of all, the loss of sight when his enemies blinded him. I am going to look at a passage from near the beginning of the speech, which covers the period before his birth, and the promises that he had apparently received regarding the divine nature of his life:

> O wherefore was my birth from Heav'n foretold
> Twice by an Angel, who at last in sight
> Of both my Parents all in flames ascended
> From off the Altar, where an Off'ring burned,
> As in a fiery column charioting
> His Godlike presence, and from some great act
> Or benefit reveal'd to Abraham's race?
> Why was my breeding order'd and prescribed
> As of a person separate to God,
> Design'd for great exploits; if I must die
> Betray'd, Captived, and both my Eyes put out,
> Made of my Enemies the scorn and gaze;
> To grind in Brazen Fetters under task
> With this Heav'n-gifted strength? O glorious strength
> Put to the labour of a Beast, debased
> Lower than bondslave! Promise was that I
> Should Israel from Philistian yoke deliver;
> Ask for this great Deliverer now, and find him
> Eyeless in Gaza at the Mill with slaves,
> Himself in bonds under Philistian yoke;
> Yet stay, let me not rashly call in doubt
> Divine Prediction; what if all foretold
> Had been fulfill'd but through mine own default?
> Whom have I to complain of but myself?
>
> (*Samson Agonistes*, ll. 23–46)

Samson contrasts his present situation with the promises which had been given before his birth, and with the instructions given to his parents to bring him up as a person dedicated to God and destined to perform great actions for his nation. What can God have meant by such preparations if the future champion was to be defeated in the end? But Samson reminds himself that his own conduct is enough to account for the apparent failure of the prophecies. The passage contains, then, the opposition between Samson's perception of his present state and his awareness that it is his own fault, not that of God, which has led him here, all of which grows from the basic opposition of the individual and order. Even at this early juncture of the text, we may see the central issues of responsibility for one's own position and the need to justify the ways of God. The interest in these opening lines arises from the balance between Samson's outcry against his fate, and his rather glib recognition of his own part in that downfall.

The passage opens with two huge questions, both of which pivot around an impression of selfishness expressed in the word 'my'. The central tension of these lines springs from the selfishness of the questioner. Note the phrases containing the possessive pronoun 'my' – 'my birth', 'my Parents', my breeding', 'my Eyes', 'my Enemies'. The second question balances on the phrase, 'if I must die', which adds strength to this catalogue of self-awareness. These are the questions of a figure who is totally caught up in himself, wrapped up in his own situation, railing against a fate which has brought him so low, yet apparently concerned only with the effect of this fate upon himself. The problem is that Samson is not truly *self-aware*, at this stage, but rather is *self-pitying*, conscious only of the terrible things that have happened to him. The force of his questions, and the phrases they contain, noted above, directs itself inwards in a way that cannot allow for the possibility of any reason behind the things which have happened. They are questions which can allow no answer, although they are not 'rhetorical questions' in which the speaker knows what the answer should be.

In the passage you might notice, too, how a simple re-ordering of syntax places the personal pronoun, 'I', at the end of line 38, thus stressing once again the egotistical quality of the material, while the *promise* itself, which attempts to broaden the scope of the complaint, collapses into the impersonal question. Again, Samson mocks the expectations he had anticipated by ironically referring to himself as 'this great Deliverer', now blind and bound to the 'Philistian yoke'. Much of this passage stresses Samson's inability to accept what has happened to him. He is impatient at his present circumstances, railing against whatever providence has brought him here, and failing to understand why this has happened. Impatience is the keynote to our understanding of Samson's growth, for it is by achieving *patience* that he eventually achieves his goal.

The whole passage, then, turns upon Samson's obsession with himself, his refusal to accept his present circumstances, his incredulity that he must blame himself for these, and, finally, his impatience that he appears to be powerless. This is where the whole poem begins, and it is from this position that we set out, in our reading, to discover how Samson is changed to the extent that he can sacrifice himself for the betterment of others. In the opening lines, the issue of patience in the face of apparently overwhelming odds is being raised very pointedly. The good man, the 'virtuous' man, is he who can bear with vicissitudes, strong in the knowledge that there is a divine plan, and that true self-knowledge is the key to the understanding of that plan. At present, Samson possesses neither strength of faith, nor self-knowledge, and is thus at the lowest point of his career. It is interesting to note that the text, even at this point, is cleverly offsetting physical and spiritual strength, which is also a powerful theme of the whole poem. Samson's impatience arises in large part from his sense of his own physical impotence – he can *do* nothing, despite his reputation as a figure of strength, because he has been stripped of that power. As a result of that impotence, he is willing to doubt providence. Yet the text is indicating clearly that what he needs to learn is spiritual forbearance, a much more potent and divinely attributable characteristic. Beyond this again the theme of patience is reflected out to the reader of the poem, who learns to accept the static nature of the whole piece as a kind of metaphor for Samson's slow journey to awareness.

At this point I am ready to move on into the poem in order to explore these ideas further.

2 Select a second passage for discussion

The following passage appears in Samson's speech which follows his discourse with his father, Manoa:

I was his nursling once and choice delight,
His destined from the womb,
Promised by Heav'nly message twice descending.
Under his special eye
Abstemious I grew up and thrived amain;
He led me on to mightiest deeds
Above the nerve of mortal arm
Against the uncircumcised, our enemies.
But now hath cast me off as never known,
And to those cruel enemies,
Whom I by his appointment had provoked,
Left me all helpless with th' irreparable loss
Of sight, reserved alive to be repeated
The subject of their cruelty or scorn.
Nor am I in the list of them that hope;
Hopeless are all my evils, all remediless;
This one prayer yet remains, might I be heard,
No long petition, speedy death,
The close of all my miseries, and the balm.

(*Samson Agonistes*, ll. 632–51)

This passage returns us to the material of the first extract. Once again, Samson recounts his thoughts about what he believed was his destiny, briefly refers to his moments of success, but then ends with his present, apparently hopeless, position. Only one thing appears to be left for him – to pray for a quick death to release him from his troubles.

An initial tension arises in these lines as we realise that Samson is addressing God, rather than his father. Initially, at least, the suggestion that he is imputing blame on Manoa is quite feasible, as he refers to himself as 'his nursling and choice delight', familiar vocabulary of the father-son relationship. That the 'father' in this case is in fact God becomes clearer as the passage moves on to Samson's career. We realise, with something of a shock, that 'He led me on to mightiest deeds' cannot refer to Manoa, and when he says 'I by his appointment' the shift has been confirmed. Samson is using the father-son vocabulary to describe what he now believes is his severed relationship with God. The central feature of the text has thus moved on to the question of filial relationships, although at this point it is more of a questioning of 'paternal relationships', as the son questions what appears to be God's rejection of him. The tenor of the whole passage suggests that Samson has now completely set aside any doubts he had at the beginning as to who should be to blame for his downfall. Nothing here indicates the possibility that he can blame himself, everything has been brought about because God has left him 'all helpless'. The passage, then, is the lowest point of Samson's impotent self-absorption, totally lacking in self-awareness, which he should be seeking. The first eight lines stress this failure by means of a vocabulary which highlights Samson's own acceptance of God's providence, while suggesting that, somehow, God was playing a kind of cruel game with him. The key phrase here is 'He led me on', which carries the sense of duplicity on the part of God; and the lines end with the two words 'our enemies', which suggest his and God's, rather than the people of Israel, and this further implies that God was using Samson to sort out His own problems.

The opposition we noted in the first extract between an impatient Samson and one who is vaguely aware that he is to blame for his own downfall has here completely disappeared. This is total impatience, as Samson rejects God, rejects solutions to his current circumstances, and, finally, rejects life. He has to learn to accept the demands of responsibility. God has not rejected him, for, if anything, it is he who now rejects God, and he will certainly compound that rejection if he seeks his own death. Filial responsibility demands an acceptance of paternal authority, and God's authority is final. This failure to perceive his role in the relationship marks the passage as Samson's ultimate mistake. Once again, he is self-pitying and selfish, and there will be no redemption for him while he remains so.

There are some interesting stylistic devices in the closing lines of this passage, which I believe add emphasis to the points I have just made. The most obvious of these is the number of repetitions of various sound patterns. There are the words containing 're-' – 'irreparable', 'reserved', 'repeated', 'remediless'; the 'loss' and 'less' sounds – 'helpless', 'loss', 'hopeless', 'remediless'; the association of these with the word 'all' on three occasions; and the reiterated first person pronouns 'I' and 'my'. This repetition seems to indicate a kind of emptiness in Samson's speech, a clamouring after language to express ideas which are without point. As a consequence, the reader tends to be left with a clutter of sounds rather than a body of meaning, and we receive the impression that this is all so much verbal whining rather than material to be listened to. The point of much of this stylistic excess is, I would say, to show the extent to which Samson has been reduced to meaningless, rather clever, babble. What he says does not convince us or himself, and it becomes a part of the developing internal dialogue that is central to the poem. Samson has, as it were, to verbalise his own doubts before he can reject them. It is almost as if the present passage is a deliberate attempt to show that these complaints are meaningless verbiage – the truth lies elsewhere.

Let us move on to a passage shortly after Samson's next encounter, with his wife Dalila.

3   Select a third passage for discussion

Perhaps surprisingly, Samson does not say too much after Dalila's departure, but there is the following brief exchange with the Chorus, which is worth a quick examination:

> *Chorus.*   She's gone, a manifest Serpent by her sting
>   Discover'd in the end, till now conceal'd.
>
> *Samson.*   So let her go; God sent her to debase me,
>   And aggravate my folly who committed
>   To such a viper his most sacred trust
>   Of secrecy, my safety, and my life.
>
> *Chorus.*   Yet beauty, though injurious, hath strange power,
>   After offence returning, to regain
>   Love once possess'd, nor can be easily
>   Repulsed, without much inward passion felt
>   And secret sting of amorous remorse.
>
> *Samson.*   Love-quarrels oft in pleasing concord end,
>   Not wedlock-treachery endangering life.
>
> > (*Samson Agonistes*, ll. 997–1009)

The Chorus announces Dalila's departure by referring to her as 'a manifest Serpent', and Samson dismisses her in a similar vein. The

Chorus then briefly wonders whether there might be some danger in her beauty which could have tempted Samson, but he scornfully rejects this idea.

What is important to my developing argument in these lines is the sense in which Samson is moving away from self-pity towards self-analysis, and revealing an acceptance of God's renewed presence in his life. The connotations of Dalila's being seen metaphorically as a serpent are numerous: perhaps the most obvious one in the context of my book is that it puts her on a plane with Satan in *Paradise Lost*. Satan, disguised as a serpent, successfully tempted Eve to eat of the fruit of the forbidden tree; Dalila, by contrast, offers a similarly fateful temptation, but is rejected by Samson. He acknowledges that he succumbed to her beguiling ways earlier on, but now he can easily dismiss her pleadings for reconciliation, and, moreover, can just as easily dismiss the temptation offered by her feminine beauty. It is the way in which Samson dismisses Dalila that has most impact on what I am saying about this figure.

In the first place, he openly states God's involvement in this episode – 'God sent her to debase me' – referring not to his earlier entrapment, but to this her most recent visit, as the next line confirms. He does not reject out of hand this divine intervention, but recognises it as a means by which he may begin to admit the centrality of his own role in his downfall. In telling Dalila the secret of his strength, Samson recognises 'my folly', but, further than this, recognises openly that what he betrayed was 'his most sacred trust' – in other words, in betraying himself to Dalila, he betrayed *God*, a serious disruption of the relationship. Moreover, that trust concerned 'my safety, and my life'. God has placed Samson in a situation in which he is responsible, by maintaining his relationship, for his own security; in breaking that trust, Samson can only be responsible for his own destruction.

This open avowal of the role he plays in God's appointed destiny for him places Samson firmly back on the path to salvation of himself, and, ultimately, the nation whose security lies in *his* hands. This point is indirectly confirmed in Samson's response to the Chorus's questioning of Dalila's power to tempt him through beauty. The two lines of his answer have much greater relevance than merely to his relationship with his wife. In terms of his relationship with God, his filial responsibility, his falling out with God as seen in the previous two extracts may perhaps be seen

for what they are – a 'love-quarrel'. The father-son relationship is
a natural one, not 'devised' as in 'wedlock', and after a quarrel
between two partners in a natural relationship there may well
come 'pleasing concord', a satisfactory conclusion. Thus Samson
uses the Chorus's doubts to reiterate two major features of his
developing self-awareness. After the encounter with Dalila, he has
begun to realise that God is still involved in his career, and he has
successfully engaged with the latest example of this. Secondly, that
relationship between himself and God demands that he recognise
his own role and responsibilities, but equally makes clear that God
is merciful, that a relationship based upon mutual love can never
be permanently damaged, as can one based upon false premises
such as was his marriage with Dalila. She might have been the
cause of his final failure, had he succumbed to her wishes or her
feminine charms, but in rebutting her temptations he has begun
the transformation of himself into a genuine figure of divine
proportions, whose strength lies in spiritual and moral concerns
rather than in physical prowess.

4   Select a fourth passage for discussion

As a last passage, I want to look briefly at Samson's speech following
his encounter with the Philistine champion, Harapha.

> He must allege some cause, and offer'd fight
> Will not dare mention, lest a question rise
> Whether he durst accept the offer or not,
> And that he durst not plain enough appear'd.
> Much more affliction than already felt
> They cannot well impose, nor I sustain,
> If they intend advantage of my labours,
> The work of many hands, which earns my keeping
> With no small profit daily to my owners.
> But come what will, my deadliest foe will prove
> My speediest friend, by death to rid me hence,
> The worst that he can give, to me the best.
> Yet so it may fall out, because their end
> Is hate, not help to me, it may with mine
> Draw their own ruin who attempt the deed.
>   (*Samson Agonistes*, ll. 1253–67)

Responding to the Chorus's fears that Harapha will complain to the Philistine Lords about his insolence, Samson makes light of any possible danger to himself. He suggests that if they ill-treat him any further they will only do themselves damage because the work that he currently does for them is worth that of many men. If they should kill him this would bring him the death he has longed for, and it may well also bring disaster upon his captors.

I think the first thing to note in this passage is the tone of Samson's speech. From the jagged, restless repetitiveness of the earlier examples, he has moved on to a calm, rational, almost dispassionate appraisal of the circumstances, leaving the agitated reaction to the Chorus. The four sentences contained in this speech are measured and careful in their syntax, using what repetition there is to emphasise a valuable point rather than cloud it in words. Equally, there is a control over the syntax which allows Samson to develop complex points without the reader losing track. This controlled tone is matched by an equally controlled content, which begins to resolve a number of the central oppositions of my exploration of this figure.

The first of those was anger and impatience over his own perceived inability to come to terms with, or control, his present circumstances. Now, Samson acknowledges that, to a large extent, he was wrong in his expectations. He has learned patience by realising that the situation will resolve itself in spite of himself, through the deeds of others which he cannot even hope to control, but which are, it is implied, subject to God's plan for his destiny. He does not fear Harapha's threats because they are either meaningless bluster, which Samson himself has now rejected, or because they are bound to be helpful to God's plan for Samson's future. The second sentence is a world away from Samson's earlier complaints, stressing how far he has come on his journey to self-awareness. Rather than howling at the terrible condition he is in, Samson quietly accepts that there is little more that the Philistines may inflict upon him, but he goes further in recognising that, even in slavery, he is valuable, and, moreover, of greater value than many men, even if that value only provides 'profit daily to my owners'.

The final two sentences begin with phrases which increasingly indicate Samson's acceptance of events as belonging to a pattern. 'But come what will' and 'Yet so it may fall out' are the words of a patient man prepared to allow that his destiny may be working itself out even though he is not totally conscious of what the end may be. Death seems to be the likeliest eventuality, yet this will no longer be the futile, despairing death that he sought earlier on; Samson now appears to be convinced that his death will have some other, greater significance, and that, in particular, it seems likely to bring about catastrophe to the Philistines, which will be the fulfilment of his destiny as was previously prophesied. By means of self-analysis, Samson has learned to control his own impatience at being apparently incapable of achieving anything positive, and can now project himself into a future that will ultimately prove his value as 'a person separate to God', as he claimed in the opening lines of the poem. The strength of Samson's newly acquired self-knowledge is reflected in the balance of ideas present in these last two sentences. The Philistines, his enemies, his 'deadliest foe', will become, through their actions, his 'speediest friend', and those actions which will be 'The worst that he can give' will prove to be for Samson 'the best'. Opposing ideas find their balance, the tension now resolving itself into a stable awareness of both ends of the spectrum. Similarly, Samson sees the destructive urges of the Philistines arising from their hatred of him, not from any wish to 'help' him, but that balanced perception will allow him to destroy them as well as himself.

II   Aspects of the text

Samson, then, has almost completed his journey to self-renewal. He is calm, reasoned, balanced and, as befits his role in God's plan, once more prophetic. He now perceives the possibilities of his own destiny and can patiently await their outcome. He knows that he will die, but that, paradoxically, his death may bring the chance of life for his people with the destruction of their captors. The one thing left for him is an understanding of the fact that the Hebrews may not benefit directly from his actions. The episodes of the text that deal with the Officer and Samson's reactions to his requests provide that opportunity. Initially Samson rejects the Officer's demands that he present himself before the Philistines to entertain them with feats of physical strength. This indicates that he has rejected mere physical powers as proof of God's having chosen him. His reason for finally accepting the Officer's request is couched in terms which indicate, as with the Dalila passage, a deeper underlying meaning than a surface reading would suggest.

> Masters' commands come with a power resistless
> To such as owe them absolute subjection
> And for a life who will not change his purpose?
>
> (*Samson Agonistes*, ll. 1404–6)

The Officer understands 'Masters' to mean the Philistine lords, but there is a clear indication for the alert reader that Samson means God. He has now accepted his filial responsibility and accepted that God's authority over him is 'absolute'. The third line of my quotation is full of all sorts of double meanings, but surely the one most indicated is the life offered by God to his supreme hero. Samson himself has 'change[d] his purpose', moving from despair and impatience to acceptance, and, therefore, hope. He will achieve his goal, even though he cannot be sure exactly how.

This tends to confirm the basic humanity of Samson as a figure in the text. Unlike the heroic Christ of the other two major works, he is a figure subject to human frailty and fallibility who has succumbed to the temptations of temporal power and feminine charm, but who, through the powers of reason and self-analysis, has been able to reassert himself. He now accepts his role in the plan God has for him and awaits, with patience, the culmination of that destiny, knowing that his death will be for the greater good of his people, although he may not know how. Earlier, Samson's impatience sprang from his not knowing why his fate had turned out in the way it had. Now, he has learned that a human has no right to question God's intentions, as they are likely to be on a plane beyond our comprehension. We must learn forbearance and suffer what appears to be a malign fate because it may be part of a plan the outcome of which is beyond our comprehension. That this is the case may be confirmed in the Chorus's speech which ends the whole poem:

> All is best, though we oft doubt,
> What th' unsearchable dispose
> Of highest wisdom brings about,
> And ever best found in the close.
>
> (*Samson Agonistes*, ll. 1745–8)

The text has shown us a figure who has learned to come to terms with this, though the learning process may be painful. God's 'uncontrollable intent' cannot be resisted, and it is the duty of mankind to accept this, not passively, but with patience, in 'peace and consolation',

> And calm of mind, all passion spent.
> *(Samson Agonistes*, l. 1758)

If we accept that *Samson Agonistes* is Milton's last composition, we may begin to see how the poet, blind and despairing at the failure of the revolution and the Commonwealth, was bringing himself and the readers who sympathised with his position to an acceptance that, after all, God's plan for humanity may yet be worked out in ways that we cannot begin to fathom. That idea is perhaps as relevant to our own age, or any other, as it was to the seventeenth century, and whether we believe in God or not, a belief in the presence of some kind of plan renders existence a little less harrowing and desperate.

Once again, my analysis of this poem has concentrated solely upon one aspect. However, as is the case all the way through this book, I hope that the method will have indicated to you how to approach *Samson Agonistes*. If you want to know more, you will have to return to the text and explore further. Keep to the text, however, certainly in the initial stages, because it is from the text itself that you will derive most pleasure and satisfaction. Milton is an endless source of delight to the careful student who is prepared to listen to what he has to say. His poems offer hours of joy, as well as, I must admit, hours of torment, but in the end the task is worthwhile. He truly is one of the great writers of the English language, and, in his own words,

> He who of those delights can judge, and spare
> To interpose them oft, is not unwise.
> *(Sonnet XVII*, ll. 13–14)

8
How to Write an Essay on Milton

There is one task which may appear to be daunting to the 'not unwise' – having studied Milton, you will probably be required to write an essay about him. This, unfortunately, is often the place where the fabric of wonderful theories comes apart in your hands. You have read a book such as this, perhaps developed the method suggested by it, brought to your text a wealth of notes and have several passages clear in your mind. Then you enter into an examination room to find yourself confronted with a question like this:

> 'In Book IV of *Paradise Lost* the ideal of nature perfectly reflects the ideal of humanity.' Discuss this view.

Your first reaction may well be, 'Where do they find these quotations?'. How can examiners pluck sentences out of some critical work like this, giving you no clue to the background of this argument or how its originator developed his ideas? Was this pithy, epigrammatic statement the conclusion to a chapter, or a book; was it the opening to an argument which actually demolished its apparent conviction; or was it merely another sentence lost in a complex argument really about something else entirely? Whatever the doubts, however, it is your task to construct an essay that uses this quotation as its starting point. So how do you do it?

There is no easy answer. What I can suggest in this chapter is one way of approaching the problem, and that is principally by means of one word – organisation. You need organisation on three levels – organise your preparation, organise your thoughts, organise your writing. Without these three you may as well not bother. Without preparation you will know nothing and can say nothing; without thought what you have to say will be shapeless and meaningless; without preparation and thought it should be pretty obvious that there can be no writing. Far too often, however, students refuse to organise themselves properly and continue in the blind belief that when the time comes for essay writing somehow there will be a magical transformation of their haphazard attitude and the words will flow onto the page, producing an essay that must stun and astonish the examiner with its felicity and brilliance. Frequently, examiners are stunned, but into a sense of disbelief that individuals can actually write in the way some students do and believe that they are saying something valuable and meaningful. So, the first thing to acknowledge is that no essay writes itself. If you are not prepared to organise your time and your approach then the end-result will be worthless. What I shall try to set out in this chapter is an explanation of my three levels of organisation, not as an infallible route to inevitable success, but as a pointer in the right direction. If you don't like my suggestions, that's up to you, but if that is the case, don't shrug your shoulders and say, 'I can't write essays'. Go somewhere else and find someone else's method of organising, and keep looking until you find one. Every book in the series to which this one belongs has a chapter like this, some more detailed than others – if you are serious about your studies, one of these must be right for you, or must be made to be right for you.

Organising an essay

1   *Organise your preparation*

It is of fundamental importance that you do not fool yourself into believing that an essay may be written without adequate preparation. What does that preparation involve? I think that it basically means a realisation of the type of essay question that may be set. Perhaps somewhat crudely, I would say that all essays on Milton are *either* going to be about character and characterisation; or about themes and issues; or about language, style and form. Nine out of ten titles may be slotted into one or more of these categories, so your preparation needs to ensure that you have an adequate understanding of how your text works in relation to them. I have tried to show you throughout this book a method of studying which explores these areas, sometimes separately, sometimes in unison. If you follow that method, going back over your text several times from different angles, you should end up with a body of material that constitutes a very good working preparation.

The first of my categories, character and characterisation, perhaps needs a little more care than the others as regards Milton's writing. I have stressed occasionally the fact that Milton's characters should not be seen as the equivalent of, say, the characters in a nineteenth-century realistic novel, but as figures who represent, in more or less detail, significant ideas within the text. Nevertheless, the vocabulary of character study may be applied to the major figures, such as Satan, or Adam, or Samson. When you are writing up your preparation I would suggest that you try to refer to these as 'figures' rather than 'characters' because it helps to maintain that sense of distance. Otherwise, you may begin to start seeing these non-human creations in human terms, which either reduces them or narrows their impact. That is why I have included the idea of characterisation in my category heading, because this is the area where you should really concentrate when you are preparing. Why does Milton describe Satan as several different things, ranging from a huge dragon-like creature on the burning sea in Hell to a cormorant when sat on the Tree of Life in Paradise? Explore your text to find answers to that question, rather than simply reject it as 'poor grasp of character'. If you are studying *Paradise Lost*, you are likely to come across the 'Satan as hero' problem at some stage. Consideration of characterisation rather than character might lead you away from what can otherwise be a troublesome, vexing question, because you should ask yourself whether the term 'hero' may justifiably be applied to this figure at all, since he appears to change shape so often. In your notes, provide yourself with a list of the 'characters' present in your text, but ensure that you append to that list plenty of material and references to how the figures are presented.

The themes and issues category is rather more straightforward. All I would say at this point is that you try to keep the ideas fairly simple in your preparatory material. Perhaps, in the end, the central issue in Milton's writing is the eternal conflict between good and evil to which all his texts may be ultimately related. Start with such a basic opposition, by all means, but make sure that you work out how other issues arise from it, and how Milton manipulates various themes which enable the reader to come to terms with these issues. It is in this category that wider critical reading can be most helpful, as long, again, as you organise this reading. By examining the text in the ways suggested in this book, you should be able to perceive the most important issues present. In order to ensure that you have come to the right conclusions, it is then worth examining critical material to find support for your views, or even to find refutations of it. Just because a critic appears to reject your viewpoint does not mean that you were wrong, but it may suggest that there are other considerations to be made which might enable you to shift your focus, or perhaps focus more sharply. This, again, is a further reason for looking initially for fairly broad issues, because if you go off looking for support for the idea that the central issue of *Samson Agonistes* is 'masculine vanity' you may be sorely disappointed to find that no one agrees with you! When you do find support, or you find a reference that substantiates your reading, make a note of it, because it may be useful either in supporting your views in an essay, or in suggesting the kind of area that might be likely to appear in an examination title.

The last category, language, style and form is always popular with examiners of Milton. As I have noted in this book elsewhere, Milton frequently experimented with form in his writing, rarely if ever returning to the same form more than once in his English poems. The sole exception to this is his use of the sonnet form, some nineteen of which exist, but even here he was responsible for creating a whole new type of sonnet which has since acquired his name. Throughout my book I have tried to point to Milton's use of form and language to reinforce or support his ideas. You will find, in your critical reading, masses of material which deals with this category, and if you are not very careful, you may be led astray into what is rightly the study of poetics rather than poetry. Milton is a rich seam for those seeking to construct, or demolish, theories of poetic style and form, but he can be a minefield for students who suddenly find themselves flung into explorations of rhetorical or classical devices. In terms of my approach, whether Milton was a poet trapped in his own extensive reading of the classical Greek and Roman authors, or a poet exhilarating in the freedoms offered by the English language, seems hardly relevant. What we do have is the poems themselves, and the student can handle the language and style of the poems quite easily as long as these aspects are seen as an entry into the much more important *ideas* they contain. You can certainly prepare yourself by carefully examining simple, obvious stylistic devices, such as Milton's use of imagery, or even his use of epic similes, for example, without becoming swamped by things like 'anacoluthon' or 'echoes of Horace'. John Peck and Martin Coyle's companion volume in this series, *Literary Terms and Criticism*, has an excellent chapter on poetry which covers most of the ground that you are likely to need. Most questions about style should arise naturally out of your reading of the text, and, as I suggested above, if you examine the characterisation of Milton's poems, you should be well on your way to understanding how he uses language and style to further his purposes.

2   *Organise your thoughts*

This is a vital part of the process of organisation which is intermediate between preparation and writing. To a certain extent, much of it cannot be done until you have seen the title of your essay. If this is in an examination, then the time for organising your thoughts may be very short indeed, and is likely to arise out of your understanding of the title itself, a point I will look at in the next section. However, if the essay you are writing is not for examination purposes, or is not constrained by a time factor, then you may have the opportunity to organise your thoughts more carefully, and to the advantage of your essay in its final shape. I suppose, in many ways, organising your thoughts before writing an essay is the same as constructing a 'plan', but I hesitate to call it that simply because, in my experience, too many students use a 'plan' as an excuse for lack of preparation, or as an attempt to convince the examiner that the badly organised mish-mash which is to follow really does have an organising mind behind it.

Thoughts about an essay arise from the preparation that has gone before, they do not emerge out of a state of panic when confronted with a title which means nothing to you. You need, first of all, to decide which of the three categories outlined in my first section best fits the title you are given. Having done that, you can turn to your notes at the relevant section and look at your material to see what, if anything, would be best in the narrow confines of the title. If you find something, all well and good; if you don't, then try to see if what you do have may perhaps be re-interpreted in such a way that it will be appropriate; otherwise, stop at this point and go back to the text itself. When you have some material to work on, I find that the best way to organise thoughts is to write them down. Given that you have the time to do this, I would suggest you write out a complete, or near complete draft of the essay, simply putting the material you have into a rough order, either as it strikes you, or, more usefully, in the order which a developing argument might suggest. You may believe that this is a part of the process of writing an essay, rather than thinking about it, but there is an important difference. Organising thought is almost impossible in the abstract. How many times have you sat at a table, text and notes open before you, and tried to engage in the process of thinking? What happens? Your mind immediately begins to wander, perhaps beginning with the subject, but very quickly disappearing down untrodden paths of irrelevance. After a given period of time, you find yourself believing that your mind is a blank or that you can't concentrate, and you abandon the 'essay' for something less taxing such as watching television. Thoughts written down on paper begin to acquire some kind of shape, and frequently the actual writing itself composes 'thoughts' which you did not realise you had. The mistake in this process is to believe that the end product of writing out your thoughts is actually the finished essay. It most certainly is not, and, again, there is little greater guarantee of annoying the examiner or reader than blithely assuming that your written thoughts constitute an 'essay'.

Time is of the essence in this part of the process. If you have the time, use it wisely. Don't anticipate being able to write out a draft, re-organise it and compose an essay in a single sitting, particularly if that is done the day or evening previous to the deadline. Writing out and organising your thoughts should take up several occasions, the more the better, particularly if you can devote time to further study in between. Milton may have claimed to have written *Paradise Lost* at the direct inspiration of the Holy Spirit, but remember, he spent nearly fifty years preparing for the writing of this poem. You are unlikely to be offered divine inspiration when writing an essay, but you still need time to work out what you are going to say.

3   *Organise your writing*

This is where everything comes together. An organised essay has a clearly defined and visible shape. The reader knows where he or she is going, because the writer knows too. I believe that the best way to organise an essay in the most general sense is to know where and when you are going to stop. If you sit down with a full pack of lined paper before you and the quaint idea that maybe you will complete every single sheet of this, you are going to be sorely disappointed for two reasons. First, and most likely, is that you won't get anywhere near it. Just try a little mathematics. A pack of paper is either a ream or a half-ream, that is 500 or 250 sheets. Say each page has thirty lines and your handwriting averages nine words per line. That makes roughly 270 words per page. If you write only one side of the paper, half a ream would mean 67,500 words! What are you writing, an essay or a book? The second reason for disappointment, and least likely, is that if you were to write that much there is every likelihood that your essay would be exceptionally tedious, repetitive and, yes, boring.

So, knowing where you are going to end presents you with a good, solid perspective. I can't predict the length of essay you are going to require, but I can suggest a tightly organised structure which will enable you to predict it. My own students, for example, will eventually have to sit an examination in which they have to write four different essays in three hours. That means roughly forty-five minutes per essay, including thinking and selecting. If I knock off five minutes for organising thoughts, that leaves forty minutes for writing. There is no way that those students will be able to provide more than about four sides of A4 in that time, given that their writing must remain legible and their thoughts coherent. Therefore, my students in their preparatory essays are asked to confine themselves to this limit. This may appear arbitrary in the extreme, but, in the end, the examination will be their judge, and the prepared, organised candidate has less to fear from 'time, the subtle thief of youth'.

Now, what do you do with those four pages, or however many you have decided is your limit? Obviously, you organise them. Again, drawing on my own students' experience, I initially shackle them to an eight paragraph, one paragraph per half page format. For weeks they squeal in agony at this apparent strait-jacket to their imaginative liberty. Eventually, however, and sooner rather than later, they begin to realise that this shape is more liberating than their so-called liberty. The unconfined anarchy of the shapeless, unstructured essay in the end leads nowhere but to the wide

pastures of waffle and drivel. My organised shape means this –
getting in, making the point, getting on, getting out. There is
no room for the pseudo-philosophical speculation about Milton's
theology, or, worse, Milton's biography. The point is this, if you
can't make clear a stage in your argument within half a page
(remember our maths, approximately 150 words), then either the
argument needs re-shaping, or the stage is not particularly obvious
or understood, or you are trying to say too much in too short a space.
Build an argument in clear, coherent, easily assimilated stages and
by the end of the essay the examiner has understood you. If your
argument is also based soundly on reference to the text then the
task is complete. In theory, you cannot go wrong!

What of the eight paragraphs then? Well, first and last there is
an introduction and a conclusion. The introduction should make
perfectly clear what the title means to you, and what you intend
to do with it. This does not mean writing out the title again, nor
starting with 'In this essay I am going to write about. . .', nor does
it mean, of course, 'Milton was a great poet who was born. . .'. It
means exactly what I have said, defining the title, and outlining your
intended approach. This is where your preparatory organisation is
most significant. Let us return to that horrifying title I began with.

'In Book IV of *Paradise Lost* the ideal of nature perfectly reflects
the ideal of humanity.' Discuss this view.

What category does this belong to? If it is not immediately obvious,
a process of elimination should leave us with themes and issues.
Having decided that, thus narrowing the focus a little, how do we
define what it says? If this is an issue, what opposition is there?
Obviously, nature and humanity. Yes, but be careful, because the
quotation suggests not a conflict, but a 'reflection'; in other words,
nature, it suggests, is used as a sort of mirror in which we see
humanity, the two therefore should be the same or similar. Do you
agree with this? Well, I would say yes, they do reflect each other –
the garden in Eden is clearly described as a perfectly fitting place
for human beings to live because it provides them with everything
they need. However, we need to return to the title now because
we have missed something. The quotation mentions 'ideals', and it
also says 'perfectly reflects'. If you have read my chapter on Book IV

of *Paradise Lost* you may remember that I examined a passage which could be relevant here. What we discovered was that the garden and Adam and Eve are certainly idealised, which fits with the first detail of the title, but that the description is mediated through the eyes of Satan, so perhaps we might question the word 'perfectly'.

Thus an argument begins to shape itself. Perhaps it is worth pointing out here that argument in an essay does not necessarily mean 'conflict', it can mean 'content' as in the 'Arguments' attached to the Books of *Paradise Lost.* When I say an argument is beginning to take shape I mean that I am beginning to see the structure of my essay filling out, because I will need to discuss 'ideal nature', 'ideal humanity', how these two 'reflect' each other, and finally, perhaps, question whether they do so 'perfectly', and if they don't what reasons can be put forward for this. Immediately, my six central paragraphs begin to define themselves – two on nature, two on humanity, one on reflection, one on 'perfectly'. The essay, in other words, has begun to fall into shape. My introductory paragraph needs simply to express all these thoughts in a rather more concise way. It may, perhaps, look something like this:

One of the central interests in *Paradise Lost* Book IV is the issue of nature and humanity. Since Milton is describing a world which existed before the Fall he attempts to present both the natural environment and the human beings themselves in as ideal a way as possible. In this world before Sin and Death arrived, nature and man were not in conflict, but in harmony, and the natural world Milton presents offers a mirror image of the humans who inhabit it. However, whether this is a 'perfect' reflection is open to question, since our vision of Paradise is seen only through the distorting eyes of Satan.

That is not perfect, but it is, I believe, crisp and to the point. From now on, the examiner should have a clear idea of what I am going to write in the rest of the essay. Moreover, I know what I am going to say also, which is perhaps more important!

Now, it is not my purpose here to compose a complete essay, but to indicate the ways in which organisation actually reduces the task to manageable proportions. As I have already said, from my thoughts about the title, and the writing of my introductory paragraph, the basic structure has already emerged. I know that I have to write six paragraphs for the central element of this essay, and those paragraphs have already made themselves clear. The final question is how to organise the individual paragraphs themselves.

We noted earlier that a convincing argument is based upon valid reference to the text. I would suggest, therefore, that you should be looking for five or possibly six pertinent quotations, one for each of your paragraphs of writing. Those quotations, it must be said, should appear at or near the beginning of each paragraph, so that what you have to say arises from the text itself, in exactly the same way my thoughts throughout this book arose from the passages I examined. There is nothing worse than tagging on a quotation to the end of a stage in an argument as some kind of 'proof' of what you have said. It is your task, remember, to show how the text gives rise to your argument, rather than to present that argument and hope that some quotation will support it. Keep your quotations fairly short, be prepared to offer fragments, rather than whole statements, which, particularly with Milton, can run into several lines of verse. Two or three lines of judicious quotation should be ample, giving far more focus to what you have to say than ten, fifteen or twenty lines of probably irrelevant material.

The first four main paragraphs constitute the essential core of your essay, and should provide the examiner with your most solid evidence that you understand the title and are debating it. Remember, you are writing the essay, not Milton, so the examiner wants to hear what you have to say rather than read large chunks of a text he or she probably knows very well already. If you are in a so-called 'closed book examination', that is, you do not have the text itself with you to refer to, then knowledge of neat, memorable quotations is going to be far better than long passages which may turn out to be entirely irrelevant. Finally on this matter, make your quotations work. Don't quote three or four lines and then appear completely to ignore them in your paragraph. Let them be an integral part of what you have to say, so that your argument builds naturally from the lines you have given. If necessary, you can give a quotation to begin with and then actually use further fragments of the same material in your analysis. Don't forget, also, that close reference to incidents in the text can be just as valuable as actual quotation because it will help to convince the examiner that you have read the text and understood it.

4   *Things to avoid*

Finally, it may be worthwhile pointing out some of the more obvious things you should avoid doing, and perhaps one or two of the less obvious ones which are easily overlooked.

When you are preparing to write an essay, never rely upon one source of information, particularly if that source is your teacher or lecturer, or, even worse, yourself. Don't spend your life reading critical books until your head is full of so many conflicting theories that it is impossible to know anything. But you can dip into other texts, as I will suggest further on. Don't approach your text with the attitude that you are going to hate this piece of writing. I have known many students who have come to Milton convinced they are going to hate him because of all the rumours they have heard from fellow students, or parents, or unsympathetic tutors. If, for some strange reason, I had to write an essay about football, which I find particularly tedious, I would at least try to set aside my dislike before I even started; I might even discover something to interest me if I was open-minded enough, but if I took to it the conviction that football is a waste of time my essay would be unlikely to succeed.

Don't try to do your preparation, or organise your thoughts in an environment that is not conducive to it. I'm not a puritan, and if you can work in a room throbbing to music then all well and good, but it might be worth trying to do it in silence, just once, to see if there is any difference. Libraries, for example, are not places of hushed reverence because of the whim of some dictatorial librarian, but because many people find it easier to work in such an environment.

Don't prepare an essay before you enter an examination room, or write the essay you wanted to write no matter what the titles given. In most cases there will be a choice in the examination, and if you have organised your preparation, one title at least will engage you. Nothing is worse for someone reading an essay than to find an initial sentence which either twists or ignores a title and then plunges off into a character study that was not required. It may well be a brilliant character study, but if the title wanted you to examine the language, it will be a brilliant waste of effort.

Avoid the utter silliness of examination room humour, such as answering the question 'Was Milton's portrayal of Samson an effective one?' with the single word 'Yes'. Don't write notes to the examiner pleading illness or ignorance or whatever. Don't write out two-page quotations followed by a single sentence of your own – knowledge of the text in isolation is of little value. Try not to spell wrongly the author's name or those of the central characters, or the titles of books or poems. Write in paragraphs, in blue or black ink with as few crossings out as possible. Sounds trivial? Imagine how you would feel, presented with several pages of unparagraphed, semi-legible handwriting in red, green or luminous ink, with passages scored out apparently with a chisel, and in which, throughout, the author is referred to as 'Milnot' or 'Jhon', and the text, undifferentiated from the remainder of the essay, appears as several variants on the form Samson Agnostices. Exaggerated, perhaps, but I have seen them all.

Conclusion

If you follow these suggestions, organising your preparation, your thoughts, and, most of all, your actual writing, then an essay should not be the frightening prospect that it may appear. It is not easy to write a good, clear essay, particularly on a notoriously difficult subject such as Milton, and I would not wish to suggest otherwise. However, the problems may be eased if you are prepared to structure your approach and severely limit yourself, particularly in the early phases of essay writing. You should be able to derive satisfaction from producing a fairly simple piece of writing that presents a cogent and coherent argument which reveals that you have seriously engaged with the text and have been seriously prepared to consider its merits.

I always tell my students that examinations should be seen as a challenge and ultimately a pleasure, because they give you an opportunity to display your knowledge, your critical ability, your ability to handle language carefully, and your joy in reading a fine piece of literature. If you make essay writing a burden, then the whole of literature becomes a tedious, joyless exercise. Milton, surely, does not deserve such an attitude, because he did not write with examinations and essays in mind. Incidentally, it may hearten you to know that my students rarely if ever accept my suggestion that examinations can be enjoyable! But I do like to believe that they take with them the glimmerings of an enjoyment in reading Milton. His writings are complex, perplexing and often appear to be divorced from what we glibly term 'everyday life', but they do present the reader with a challenge in both form and content, and there is a tremendous exhilaration to be gained from following the sheer exuberance of a body of poetry that is probably without parallel in the whole of English literature.

Further Reading

The whole point of this book is to try to encourage you to read Milton and little else. There is an industry of Milton criticism, producing countless volumes which are often of interest only to their authors. You cannot get away from some of these eventually, but I must strongly advise you only to start your further reading when you have begun to exhaust your own thoughts, gained from successive readings of the poems themselves. Milton means something different to different people at different times, and has done so throughout history since his life in the seventeenth century. That meaning, however, must come from the texts, not from somebody else's opinion of them, because, in the end, you are the reader and he wrote for you.

What I can suggest here are some of the more readily available and readily accessible books which may assist you in deepening your understanding or broadening your enjoyment. When I was a student myself, biographies seemed to be the most important things to read, and my friends and I could talk for hours about the most ludicrous details of writers' lives, while their poems or novels lay unread on the shelves. Fortunately, I was able to rid myself of this habit, and return to the real source of pleasure, which is literature itself. Nevertheless, the perspectives of other commentators can have their value, even if they appear to be running completely counter to your own. One serious generalisation I would make is always to read the latest published material first. That is not a vain attempt to put my own name forward for the microsecond in history when it may be attributable to me, but rather to stress the fact that the most recent thinking is more likely to be in tune with your own and will therefore best represent your own interpretation of the text. Reading something published in the 1930s, for example, will present you with a Milton almost unrecognisable today, slated for his language and versification, and guilty of the most peculiar sort of conservative, narrow-minded Christian puritanism. On the other hand, of course, 'Milton the revolutionary' may be the

more contemporary viewpoint, but who is to say how long that
will last?

Texts of the poems

My own 'bible of Milton' is the Oxford Standard Authors edition
of the *Poetical Works*, edited by Douglas Bush. I like it because it
is unencumbered with other than minor notes mostly devoted to
vocabulary, the editor's introductions are interesting (although
occasionally infuriating!), and the poems are presented with
modern spellings and punctuation. In hardback or paperback,
this is a book that is easy to handle and to read.

The so-called 'standard working edition' of the poems is the
Longman two volume *Complete Shorter Poems* edited by John Carey
and *Paradise Lost* edited by Alastair Fowler. These are massive
volumes, even in paperback, and occasionally can even be found
bound into a single edition of frightening dimensions. They are
erudite works of profound scholarship with copious notes and
references, but unfortunately these tend to swamp completely the
poems themselves, and you can't help but end up reading the notes
and ignoring the two or three lines of the poem which are often all
that appear on a page.

There are also innumerable editions of single Books of *Paradise
Lost* prepared for students of Milton, but they are rarely as helpful
as they set out to be. In the end, a complete text is much more
useful.

Biographies

There are, surprisingly perhaps, only a very few real biographies
of Milton, and of these most are only available in libraries. One
that should be accessible is A. N. Wilson's *The Life of John Milton*
first published in 1983, and available in paperback from Oxford
University Press. If you know little or nothing of the life of
Milton or of the history of the seventeenth century this makes
a good, interesting introduction. It reads well, is fluent and fairly
comprehensive. Its major fault is that Wilson tends to be very
conservative about Milton's political involvements, which I find

distorts the overall picture. The so-called definitive biography is W. R. Parker's *Milton: a Biography*, two volumes of immense learning, published in 1968, again by Oxford University Press. This is vast and thorough, but, in the end, perhaps, rather tedious. My own favourite is Christopher Hill's *Milton and the English Revolution*, first published by Faber in 1977. This is a combined critical analysis of the poetry and prose, biography and exploration of the historical context. It is very dense and takes some reading, but provides an overall picture which is quite unmatched in my opinion.

Criticism

I can only hope to scratch the surface here, and I do not really wish to do otherwise. Apart from texts which are similar to mine in scope and size, I would recommend only three out of the hundreds of critical works available. These texts may reveal more about my prejudices than anything else, but for the student coming new to Milton they should help to widen your understanding of the huge debate that Milton always provokes. One of my oldest favourites is C. S. Lewis's *A Preface to Paradise Lost*, first published in 1942. This is essentially a collection of lectures on the poem, much of the time concerned with the nature of epic poetry, but all of the book is provoking and interesting to read, despite its age. Next is William Empson's *Milton's God*, published by Cambridge University Press in 1961, which is a wonderfully wayward piece of writing that continually leads you to fury or pleasure. Last, but not least, a very recent book, Catherine Belsey's *John Milton, Language, Gender, Power*, published by Blackwell in 1988, is worth the struggle of reading for the splendid ways in which it changes perspectives on Milton's writing, turning over easily accepted views and inspiring new thinking.

A small collection of criticism such as this should provide you with as much stimulation and as many ideas as you need. They will, however, only make sense if you have first done your own work on Milton's texts.